THE ABSENTEE AMERICAN

THE
ABSENTEE
AMERICAN

Repatriates' Perspectives
on America

CAROLYN D. SMITH

ALETHEIA
Publications

Library of Congress Cataloging-in-Publication Data

Smith, Carolyn D.
    The absentee American : repatriates' perspectives on America
/ Carolyn D. Smith
            p.   cm.
    Includes bibliographical references and index.
    ISBN 0-9639260-0-4
    1. Americans--Foreign countries. 2. Return migration--United
States. 3. United States--Emigration and immigration.   I. Title.

First published in 1991

Aletheia Publications, 38-15 Corporal Kennedy St., Bayside, NY 11361
Cover design by Guy J. Smith

Printed in the United States of America

10 9 8 7 6 5 4 3 2 1

For Guy

CONTENTS

PREFACE

This book is based on responses to a questionnaire distributed among a sample of American adults who lived outside the United States as children because their families were living overseas, and then returned and settled here (although some subsequently went overseas again for varying lengths of time). The questionnaire explored the experiences, feelings, attitudes, and opinions of these Americans, whom I have labeled Absentee Americans to distinguish them from expatriates and from Americans who have not lived overseas. More than 300 people responded to the questionnaire, which was mailed to former students at overseas and international schools located in Kenya, Pakistan, Vietnam, Thailand, Brazil, Germany, and elsewhere, and to members of organizations such as Global Nomads International and Overseas Brats. Additional information was obtained from telephone interviews.

The individuals who responded to the questionnaire and/or were interviewed cover a wide age range—from about twenty to over seventy—although most are in their thirties or forties. The majority have been living in the United States continuously for ten or more years, that is, since entering college. For the most part, their families lived in other countries as representatives of the United States—in the Foreign Service or the military—or of private organizations, primarily churches and corporations (such as airlines and oil companies). Others were employed by the United Nations, educational institutions, or foundations.

All but a small percentage of the individuals who supplied information for this book are white, middle-class Americans. Although a number of respondents indicated that they were nonwhite or bicultural, the sample was not large enough to make it possible to distinguish these influences from the effects of growing up in a non-native environment. Nor is it possible to construct a typology of Absentee Americans—military versus nonmilitary background, childhood spent in Europe versus childhood spent in Third-World countries, and so forth. Although there are some important differences among these subgroups, they are outweighed by the similarities.

What all respondents share is the experience of having spent some or all of their formative years as an American in a country or countries other than the United States. That experience, even if brief, tends to give the Absentee American an outsider's perspective on the United States. This effect varies in intensity, but it is strikingly evident in the comments of returnees who lived overseas for as little as one year. It is as if they have stepped through a doorway and then back, and from that time on they carry with them the knowledge that the door is there and that there is a vast human universe on the other side.

What, then, is an Absentee American? An Absentee American is a person who spent part of his or her childhood outside the United States and then reentered American society, usually in the mid- to late teenage years. These individuals are referred to in other publications by various names, including "global nomads," "overseas brats," and "third-culture kids." I use the phrase

"Absentee American" to emphasize that I am referring to a special category of Americans, those who have been absent but have returned. I also use the words "returnee" and "repatriate." (Americans living abroad, even temporarily, are referred to as "expatriates." The term "repatriate" is used to indicate an expatriate who has returned to the United States to live.)

My own experiences and conversations with others from similar backgrounds led me to believe that Absentee Americans tend to share a distinctive set of attitudes and opinions regarding American society and culture that have been colored by the experience of living outside the country during childhood. This belief was confirmed by the responses of those who answered the questionnaire or agreed to be interviewed. Some clear traits and trends can be seen in their comments, and these constitute the generalizations that form the texture of this book. At the same time, it remains true that there is immense variety in the opinions and attitudes reported by Absentee Americans. Moreover, the views expressed by these individuals obviously are not unique to repatriated Americans. One does not have to live overseas in childhood to believe that the United States needs to play a more cooperative role in world affairs. It is just more likely that this will form part of the constellation of beliefs and opinions that is characteristic of Americans who have viewed the United States from the outside.

This book does not attempt to explain in detail the psychological makeup of repatriates; other writers with the appropriate qualifications have studied this subject extensively and continue to do so; some of their writings are listed in the Bibliography. Nor is this a critique of U.S. foreign policy, although returnees often commented on specific policies. It is, quite simply, a description of a particular set of experiences and attitudes, along with some of their implications. As much as possible, returnees' comments are presented in their own words.

Many respondents wrote at great length on the questionnaire and in accompanying letters. Often they thanked me for providing an opportunity for self-exploration and a chance to express opinions that in many cases had been bottled up for years. To them I can only say that the debt is mine. It has been an indescribable privilege to be allowed to share the thoughts and feelings of so many people who, like me, have stepped through the door and back.

ACKNOWLEDGMENTS

Many individuals and organizations contributed to this book in a variety of ways. First and foremost, of course, are the hundreds of repatriates who took the time to respond to the questionnaire or to answer questions by phone; they are the backbone of this book, and I am deeply grateful to all of them. I would also like to thank Vernon Boggs, William Kornblum, Joel Bryan, and Ralph Doggett for their suggestions and assistance in developing the questionnaire. Major Glen Hawkins of the U.S. Army Center of Military History, Dr. William Slany, Public Affairs Historian of the U.S. Department of State, and personnel at the Foreign Service Institute library, the Overseas Briefing Center, the Office of Overseas Schools, and the Family Liaison Office provided valuable assistance in my search for background information. Sherry Tousley, Peter Nelson, Clinton L. Doggett, Jr., William Robb, Katherine Hagen, and William Kornblum read all or part of the manuscript and offered many useful suggestions. I would also like to thank Clyde Austin, Joe Condrill, Norma

McCaig, and David Pollock for their encouragement.

1

AMERICANS ABROAD

In the decades since World War II, increasing numbers of American citizens—civilians as well as military personnel—have been stationed in countries outside the United States as representatives of the U.S. government. Many others have gone overseas on behalf of private organizations, especially churches and corporations. Beginning in the late 1940s, numerous advisers were sent to Europe, and then to Asia, Africa, and South America, as part of the U.S. foreign aid program. Established U.S. air carriers provided advisers to assist in the training of personnel for fledgling national airlines like Pakistan International Airways. The Ford Foundation, the U.S. Information Agency, oil companies, universities—all have sent personnel to other countries for a wide range of purposes.

Perhaps the most familiar of these sponsoring organizations is the Foreign Service. Although the United States has had a foreign service since 1781, when the Continental Congress created the Department of Foreign Affairs, the modern foreign service was established in 1924 by the Rogers Act, which provided a permanent career service to represent the nation abroad. The number of Americans assigned overseas increased steadily during the next two decades, but the most dramatic growth occurred after World War II. Spurred by the nation's superpower status—as well as by the Foreign Service Reform Act of 1946, which provided for the recruitment of economists and other professionals in addition to "diplomatic generalists"—the number of overseas personnel doubled, growing to more than 7,000 by 1968. Added to these were other U.S. civilian employees, for a total of almost 15,000 in the mid-1960s. Since the 1960s the number of "direct-hire" personnel stationed abroad has tended to remain constant, but the number of individuals indirectly working for the State Department or the Agency for International Development—usually employed by consulting firms—has increased significantly. The increase in Americans stationed abroad has occurred despite an actual decrease in the number of overseas posts, which peaked at 413 in 1920.

The State Department does not, of course, account for all, or even most, of the Americans living overseas. Military personnel are stationed at bases around the world, not only as members of combat and supporting troop units but as advisers to their counterparts in host countries. The Central Intelligence Agency, the U.S. Information Agency, the Peace Corps, the Departments of Treasury, Commerce, Interior, and Agriculture, and other agencies of the government also send representatives abroad. Since 1946, therefore, when it was unusual for Americans to live overseas unless they were missionaries or diplomats, it has become commonplace for American military and civilian employees and businesspeople to be stationed abroad, if only for a year. The 1990 Census counted 922,000 federal workers and their families living overseas, and the total number of Americans living abroad either permanently or temporarily is estimated at 3 million.

A large proportion of Americans who go overseas are accompanied by their families, and many have children while they are stationed abroad. During the 1950s and 1960s a whole generation of American children grew up in other countries, and they were succeeded by new generations as the interdependence of nations increased. As Louise Winfield writes in *Living Overseas*:

> As recently as 1946 the movement of American families to other parts of the world was an uncommon phenomenon, limited for the most part to missionaries, to diplomats, to certain business people, and to a relatively small number of Army and Navy families. At the present time it would be hard to find a city neighborhood or a rural community that doesn't count among its former residents people who are now living in foreign countries.[1]

Information on the actual number of families with dependent children stationed overseas at any given time is difficult to come by and for the most part consists of rough guesses. It is estimated, however, that today there are between 15,000 and 20,000 dependent children in the Foreign Service alone. The number of dependent children in the armed services overseas is quite large; enrollment at the 269 Department of Defense schools (more than half of which are located in Germany) totaled more than 150,000 in 1989–90. It is estimated that nearly a quarter of a million school-age American children are currently living overseas and that since the 1940s as many as 700,000 American teenagers have attended high school overseas.

OVERSEAS SCHOOLS

American children attend approximately 600 schools outside the United States, with enrollments ranging from as few as ten students to as many as 6,000. Children of civilian personnel generally attend independent schools that have been established on a cooperative basis by U.S. citizens living in foreign communities; these are known as "American schools." Many of these schools receive assistance from the U.S. government and are described as "American-sponsored," although they are open to nationals of all countries and their teaching staffs are multinational. Today there are 176 such schools located in 106 countries, with a total enrollment of about 93,000, of whom about 24,000 are U.S. citizens. Although the language of instruction is English and the curricular patterns are American, an effort is made to supplement the standard curriculum with quality foreign-language and local-culture programs.

The following description of the Cairo American College depicts a typical overseas school at a larger post:

> CAC, founded in 1945, is a private, coeducational day school serving students in kindergarten through grade 12. The curriculum is that of a general, college-preparatory public school in the U.S. Eighty percent of the faculty are U.S. citizens. The student body of about 1,100, approximately half of whom are American, represents 51 countries. Classes average 15 students.[2]

As noted earlier, children of military personnel attend schools operated by the Department of Defense; these are known as "U.S. Department of Defense Dependents Schools" or DODDS. They are public schools operated with tax funds on a tuition-free basis and are provided exclusively for dependents of the overseas armed forces; they are very similar to the schools found in towns and small cities in the United States. The DODDS system has been in existence since 1946, when there were only about 3,000 students attending army and air force schools.

In addition to the overseas schools sponsored by the State Department or the military, there are numerous private "international schools" operated by members of the expatriate community in cities with large numbers of American, Canadian, and British expatriates. Many children of employees of private businesses attend such schools. There are also missionary children's schools in some rural or suburban locations; many of their students live in campus dormitories or boarding homes. The Rift Valley Academy in Kenya is typical of such institutions; children of missionary families come to the school from all over Africa.

Another form of education among Americans assigned to remote or lonely posts is the correspondence course—examples include the venerable Calvert course and the University of Nebraska correspondence courses. A small minority of American children attend schools of the host country.

LIVING ARRANGEMENTS

Americans assigned overseas by the State Department may benefit from a variety of other services, such as health units, mail service, a system for finding employment for family members, and various allowances—for living quarters, cost of living, "hardship posts," and the like. At many posts direct-hire employees are assigned to permanent housing in furnished villas or apartments owned or leased by the government. (In Cairo, for example, the embassy owns and operates three apartment buildings.) Most military families also can avail themselves of numerous services and benefits; in fact, some military bases are not very different from communities in the United States, with facilities that may include stores, hospitals, chapels, and recreational facilities. Employees of private businesses and nonprofit organizations, on the other hand, must depend on whatever facilities are available in the host country.

A "THIRD CULTURE"?

Typically, Foreign Service and military personnel are sent abroad for a specified tour of duty, usually two years in the Foreign Service, three in the military. At each post they form a miniature American community, working and socializing with one another to varying degrees. They form clubs, establish schools for their children, bring in movies and records from the States, shop at the American-run post exchanges (PXs) and commissaries, and often live in the same neighborhoods and apartment buildings. This is not to say that they cut themselves off from the society in which they are living. Many Americans work closely with members of the host society, and there are numerous intercultural activities and social events. Indeed, Americans living overseas have been described as an "interstitial culture."

Living as they do between two cultures during the most formative years of their lives, the children of Americans overseas cannot help but be affected by their experiences. Indeed, in recent years sociologists and psychologists have devoted increasing attention to the effects of growing up abroad, moving frequently, and returning to the United States during adolescence. There is a growing literature on such subjects as "reverse culture shock," "continuing reentry stress," "reacculturation," and "the repatriate syndrome." The impact of growing up overseas has also become a matter of concern to the State Department and other agencies of the U.S. government. Since the mid-1970s special attention has been devoted to the difficulties accompanying the transition to life back home, or "reentry," as it is typically called. The Overseas Briefing Center of the Foreign Service Institute and the State Department's Family Liaison Office, for example, provide workshops and publications for families returning to the United States from overseas assignments, with special emphasis on teenage reentry problems. (Reentry is described in some detail in Chapter 3.)

Americans who have shared this experience are the subject of this book. They are a varied group, as can be seen from the following brief descriptions:

Nancy Young Blackmore: Student at the Harvard Graduate School of Education/Administration. Lived in São Paulo, Brazil from 1963 to 1968, in Uganda from 1972 to 1973, and in Kenya from 1973 to 1974; her father was a professor of agricultural economics working on USAID contracts. Grew up speaking Portuguese, was bilingual when she returned to the United States. Does not feel well integrated into American society.

Shannon Haycox: Homemaker. Her father worked on pineapple plantations in Hawaii, the Philippines, and Kenya. Returned to the United States at the age of eighteen; found reentry "very traumatic." On the surface, is well integrated into American society, but on another level feels as though she is from outer space.

Michael Karian: Instructor/student. Lived in Thailand between the ages of six and eleven, in Kenya from age twelve to age eighteen. Says "reentry" to the United States was actually "entry"; still feels different and plans on traveling and working overseas whenever possible.

Laura Schlesinger Minor: AIDS educator. Spent her teenage years in Nairobi, Kenya, where her father set up a technical school to train printers. After being snubbed because of her overseas background, learned not to mention it. Has a global perspective on problems like hunger, poverty, and public health.

Chuck Tigue: Computer training specialist. Son of an Air Force mess sergeant, lived in Seville, Spain during his teenage years; participated equally in the American and Spanish communities, sampling the best of both cultures. Was treated as if he was from the moon when he went to Oklahoma State University, but feels well integrated into American society now.

Sherry Tousley: College instructor, intercultural consultant and trainer. Daughter of a U.S. Army officer; lived in fifteen different places before age eighteen, including France, Germany, and Mexico. Felt a loss of excitement, status, identity, and adventure upon returning to the United States; longs to live abroad again.

Diane Rydell Anderson: Customer service agent for Trans World Airlines. Spent her teenage years in Burma, India, and Pakistan. Felt out of place upon returning to the United States and still feels different—only now feels that her differentness is an asset rather than a liability.

Peter Nelson: Intercultural trainer. Son of a Pan American World Airways executive; spent much of his childhood in Syria, the Belgian Congo (now Zaire), and Pakistan. Feels integrated into American society but would go overseas "in a heartbeat."

Andy Howell: Officer in the U.S. Air Force. Son of a career Air Force officer; attended high school in Weisbaden, Germany, where he participated in school activities much as he would have at any school in the United States. Believes that living overseas made him better able to understand how other countries perceive the United States.

Patricia Wood Goff: Accountant. Born in India of missionary parents. Believes that the United States should use its wealth and strength to help others in need, but never to dominate or control; considers herself a world citizen.

These and others like them are the Absentee Americans; they have also been called "global nomads," "overseas brats," and "third-culture kids." The term "third culture," coined by sociologist Ruth Useem, refers to the values, life-styles, and interaction patterns created and maintained by people who cross societal boundaries as representatives of a sponsoring organization, as distinct from refugees, tourists, and immigrants. John Useem explains this term as follows (referring to the situation of Americans in India):

The "first culture" indicates the patterns embedded in Indian society which are manifest among those segments of Indians who regularly interact with Americans. The "second culture" refers to corresponding patterns of American society which are incorporated in the segments of that society who live and work in India. By the "third culture" is meant the patterns which are created, shared, and learned by [members] of the two different societies who are personally engaged in the process of linking their societies, or sections thereof, to each other.[3]

Sociologist David Pollock has devoted considerable study to the personality and psychological adjustment of "third-culture kids," or TCKs. His definition of a TCK is, "An individual who, having spent a significant part of the developmental years in a culture other than the parents' culture, develops a sense of relationship to all of the cultures while not having full ownership in any. Elements from each culture are incorporated into the life experience, but the sense of belonging is in relationship to others of similar experience."[4] Pollock's profile of a TCK depicts a person with well-developed linguistic and communicative abilities, cross-cultural skills, and a larger view of the world than is typical of most Americans. Other researchers have found that TCKs tend to cope rather than adjust, and that they are both "a part of" and "apart from" any situation in which they find themselves.

In the following chapters these and other characteristics of Absentee Americans are explored in detail, with particular reference to their long-term influence on the repatriated American's perspective on the United States and its place in the contemporary world. Although some of these characteristics may also be seen in individuals who have lived overseas for the first time as adults, they take on a special intensity in repatriates who spent much of their childhood outside the United States.

NOTES

1. Louise Winfield, *Living Overseas* (Washington, D.C.: Public Affairs Press, 1962).

2. U.S. Department of State, *Egypt Post Report*, April 1990, p. 12.

3. John Useem, "Work Patterns of Americans in India," *Annals of the American Academy of Political and Social Sciences, 368* (1966): 147.

4. David C. Pollock, "Transition Experience: A Model of Reentry," unpublished manuscript, October 1987. Available from D. C. Pollock, Rt. 1, Box 23, Centerville Rd., Houghton, NY 14744.

2

LIFE OVERSEAS

Total uprootedness is contrary to our nature, and the human plant once plucked from the ground tries to send its roots into the ground onto which it is thrown.
                                                                    —Czeslow Milosz
I would never trade my experience of living overseas for all the tea in China.

The nature of life overseas varies from one post to another and from one family to another, and there are significant differences between such experiences as living on a military base, attending a boarding school, or growing up in a remote area of India or Africa. Such differences are reflected in the fact that the children of Americans overseas are often labeled according to their parents' sponsors: "army brats," "missionary kids," "biz kids," "oil kids." Nevertheless, there are some general similarities of experience that distinguish Absentee Americans from their counterparts who have not lived overseas. Those common experiences have a lot to do with the feelings and attitudes of repatriates long after they have returned to the United States. And although the living arrangements of military families tend to be different from those of Foreign Service, missionary, and other American families overseas, children from all of these groups usually spend a great deal of time together and form a community of their own.

For American children living on military bases in places like Wiesbaden, Germany, participation in the life of the American community is almost total. They have been described as living in an American "cocoon." School activities, the Girl and Boy Scouts, the Teen Club (an after-school hangout with ping-pong, jukebox, etc.), Little League, and other organized activities occupy most of their time. Although they may study the language of the country in which they are stationed, they have few opportunities to use it in everyday conversation. They may also attend cultural events such as festivals and theatrical performances, and travel and sightsee extensively, but for the most part they are discouraged by peers from interacting with host country nationals.

Not all military families live on base, but they do tend to congregate in certain areas. A returnee who lived in Morocco reports that his family lived over twenty-five miles from the base. "We commuted by school bus morning and afternoon, and had no way to get back home if we missed the bus, so we very rarely stayed on base after school. There were two busloads of kids (all grades) living in Fedala, so we had quite a few families there. Those families created an American community that was centered, from my perspective, around the Sunday school. Other involvement [in the community included] Boy Scout activities and the annual Fourth of July party at the consulate in Casablanca."

Foreign Service families are not concentrated in a single area, but they often live in the same neighborhoods or even in the same apartment buildings. They may also live in "foreign" (British, Canadian, European) apartment buildings. (The latter are not intentionally segregated; the separation is largely a matter of economics.) In Third-World countries Americans may live with two or three other foreign families in a walled compound. Adult social life tends to center on events such as Fourth of July picnics, receptions and cocktail parties, and outings with other American families. In many posts there is an American Club or recreation center. Some families make an effort to socialize with members of the host society, usually neighbors and people associated in some way with the embassy or other U.S. agencies; their children are more likely to make friends with host country children.

LIVING "ON THE ECONOMY"

Absentee Americans often describe the practice of living among members of the host society as living "on the economy." Thus, Chuck Tigue reports that "in Seville in the early sixties, one had a choice of life-styles. One extreme was to ignore the fact that you were no longer in the United States and have minimal contact with the Spaniards. In this mode, you never ventured into 'the economy' and your world was the air base and the American housing area. The other extreme was to 'go native.' These people lived 'on the economy' and blended into the scenery."

Tigue notes that the American enclave could just as well be referred to as a barrio or ghetto. Another repatriate echoes this thought: "My parents were often critical of what they described as the overseas American ghetto mentality, the tendency to live and move in totally American circles. [They] chose to move outside the American community and always made an attempt to learn about the country and culture they were living in." As these comments suggest, the attitudes of parents toward the host culture may be the most significant influence on the daily lives of American children overseas.

Some Americans living "on the economy" make an effort to create an American community *in absentia*, though it may be blended with some elements of the host country culture. They view themselves as visitors to the host country, not as permanent residents, and feel that it is important to remain rooted in American traditions. As one returnee explains, "Our situation in the Philippines was somewhat unique in that we lived in an isolated and relatively self-contained community which in the early years was all American and then gradually became integrated with Filipino families. All the families made a concerted effort to maintain, as much as possible, a normal American life-style. Committees were formed to organize parties for all the major holidays, most of which were also celebrated by the Filipinos. Thanksgiving was an exception. Because it was not a Philippine holiday and it was one that was usually spent with one's family, most people simply had a special meal with their immediate family or good friends."

An "old China hand" offers a similar description of Americans living in Shanghai during the 1930s: "We took very much for granted that we were *Americans* who happened to be living in China. We were very much a part of the Oriental world, but lived in a 'little America' inside our compound walls. There was no intention of shutting China out; my father was totally immersed in the Chinese world—spoke fluently, dealt almost entirely with Chinese, and was very comfortable in his role. We had many Chinese friends."

SCHOOL AND SOCIAL LIFE

In most military and Foreign Service communities, the school is the center of social life for American children and teenagers. For children from military families there are the DODDS schools, which are very similar to schools in the United States. In places where schools have not been established, children may meet daily to work on correspondence courses with the help of teachers (usually parents); these informal schools may evolve into a full-fledged overseas school.

Parents and school administrators often go to great lengths to organize school-related activities such as sports teams—including cheerleaders and varsity letters—as well as various types of clubs (glee club, debate club, bridge club, etc.), publications such as yearbooks and school newspapers, and parties (including senior proms) that resemble as much as possible their counterparts in the United States. Although children of many other nationalities may be found among the student body, by and large the schools are modeled on American public schools—with an added cultural fillip provided by courses in subjects like traditional Japanese dance.

The size of the schools attended by Absentee Americans varies widely. For example, in 1961 the author was one of fourteen graduating seniors at the Karachi American School. In contrast, at present the twenty-fifth largest U.S. school district is located in West Germany. During the 1960s the International School in Bangkok was the largest international school in the world, with almost 1,000 high school students on its main campus.

Rarely do Americans stationed overseas send their children to local public schools. Those who do tend to do so as part of an explicit desire to become immersed in the local culture. One returnee reports that upon arrival in Kenya all five children in her family were given six weeks of intensive training in Swahili and then attended a Kenyan school for one year. Another comments: "Since my father regarded himself as an 'international' civil servant, attempts were made not to be absorbed by the American community. However, we did enroll in the American schools after short stints with local education." Families stationed in Europe or South America are more likely to send their children to local schools than families stationed in Africa or Asia.

Children in missionary families are often sent to boarding schools such as those at Woodstock and Kodaikanal in India. Like children on military bases, they associate almost entirely with others from similar backgrounds. When they return to their families, however, they are likely to be isolated from other Americans, since missionary families often live in the countryside or in towns and villages at some distance from the cities where most Americans are stationed. The following account describes the life-style of one such family: "We lived with the local natives [in Mali] in a mud house my father built. We would travel to native villages and live for weeks with them, eating their food and working with them. Of course there were no other white kids, no radio, no electricity and none of the devices run by it. We did have a gas lamp and a typewriter, and I recall listening to the Voice of America on my father's battery-powered short-wave radio."

Even in the large cities Americans may find conditions considerably more rustic than those they have been used to in the United States. Drinking water may have to be boiled; water for bathing and laundry may be rationed. (Some posts are explicitly referred to as "boiled water posts.") There may be large insects and other unsavory creatures running around. Air conditioning is not something that can be taken for granted. In some places electricity is rationed or is turned off for hours or days at a time. The *Egypt Post Report* alludes to these conditions with a mixture of resignation and hopefulness: "The Cairo area is deficient in both the quality and extent of utilities. Frequent electrical outages, insufficient and erratic water pressure, and sewage problems occur. These are all, however, improving slowly."[1]

Because of these and other disadvantages, some places are officially designated as "hardship posts"; a favorite pastime of repatriates is trading stories about such hardships. To take just one example: "Milk came over [to Morocco] from the U.S. frozen; it took weeks to get there. When thawed, it was curds and whey; we had to heat the milk and push the curds through a strainer to try to get them broken up enough to remix with the milk. We drank a lot of instant milk, too, and sometimes we'd eat the frozen milk without thawing it, with pancake syrup poured over it."

To some extent, participation in an American community overseas is a function of the size of the community. As one returnee points out, "In Brazil and British Guiana we had many local friends and did not live the Americanized life we did in Southeast Asia. In Southeast Asia there were a lot more Americans and the 'little America' concept ruled—American school, theater, bowling alley, PX, commissary." In some places there may actually be several American communities, each with a different characteristic life-style. There is also likely to be an "international" or expatriate community whose children tend to associate with one another despite language barriers.

Children in missionary families are most likely to become immersed in the local culture and to attend host country schools. Their families travel extensively throughout the country, often taking the children along. One returnee who grew up in Kenya, Uganda, and South Africa reports that she went to African churches in the bush and participated in some tribal ceremonies. Such children are also more likely to eat local foods, wear ethnic dress, and learn the host country's language.

LANGUAGE AND CULTURAL EXCHANGE

Most Absentee Americans learn one or more foreign languages while overseas. At the very least, they learn enough words and phrases to get around town and deal with shopkeepers—although often they learn a pidgin version of the host country language (e.g., "Taxi Thai") plus the basic cuss words. A typical returnee reports, "I learned a second language in each country we lived in. My parents required us to take lessons. I only became fluent in Spanish and French, but could make myself understood (in a primitive way) in Farsi, Arabic, and Thai." Often various members of the household staff informally teach American children. In addition, the overseas schools include host country languages in their curricula.

Some young children learn other languages before they learn English, and a few become bilingual. Children who live outside the American community usually become fluent in the host country's language, and for those who spend most of their time with members of the host culture, their language may come to feel more "natural" than English. One returnee comments: "Since I spoke Portuguese like a native, I was more comfortable being like a Brasileiro. We often played soccer, hunted birds, and ate beans and rice off the same plate."

A repatriate who lived in Thailand during his teenage years comments on the importance of language: "While in Bangkok my cook at home was learning English so we helped each other with our native tongues. I personally found it frustrating to see all the street signs, store signs, advertising, etc. in a language and alphabet I didn't know, so part of my self-education was to learn to read and write the Thai language. Because of this I could penetrate the Thai culture more than the average person. The Thais—being gracious by nature—opened themselves up to me even more than normal because of my initiative to understand their language and culture."

Language often becomes part of the consciousness of Absentee Americans, as can be seen in the following example: "We sometimes watched local television programming, and, at the movies, had fun comparing the Portuguese subtitles with the American dialogue. Conversation amongst ourselves was often a mix of both languages. Our Portuguese conversations often incorporated the occasional American slangword; when speaking English, we invariably used 'untranslatable' and/or common Brazilian words. By the time we'd been in the country a while, many of us realized that even conversations in our dreams were in Portuguese!"

Travel is an important feature of the lives of most families stationed overseas. Vacation trips, safaris, and tours of places of historical or cultural interest are frequent. ("We went to every known museum, chateau, and monument," says one returnee.) The foreign post may serve as a base for longer trips; returnees often say that they traveled "all over Europe" or "throughout Africa."

Families stationed abroad are also likely to go to restaurants, movie theaters, discos, and other entertainment facilities in the host country. Almost inevitably, Absentee Americans learn to appreciate the cuisine of the countries in which they are stationed (although at the same time they often express longing for such items as soft bread and McDonald's). They also develop, to varying degrees, immunity to the local intestinal parasites that are the plague of tourists. As one repatriate remarks, "My mother would get upset thinking we would get Bangkok belly—us kids? Never!"

A few Absentee Americans comment that they tried to steer a middle course between involvement in the social life of the

American school and the culture of the host country. Chuck Tigue, for example, says, "I had school and its extracurricular activities like athletics and scholastic clubs. For social activities there was the Teen Club. But I also waded into the Spanish culture. I shopped in Seville, I bought lottery tickets, I went to billiard halls, I got drunk in cheap bars where almost no Americans would go, I went to the bull fights, I went to the museums and art galleries, I drank the water (a major no-no), I went to the horse shows/sales, I learned the spoken Spanish language and I went to the fairs." This type of experience is also common among bicultural children, whose parents often arrange to be stationed in the country in which, for example, one spouse's parents still reside.

This pattern is by no means universal. In fact, there is a rather distinct dichotomy among Americans overseas in their attitudes toward the host country. One group accepts the power outages, the traffic snarls, and the bureaucratic bungling as simply "part of the character" of the place and moves on to find things to appreciate. The other group goes beyond complaining about local conditions and finds every opportunity to make derogatory comments about the character of the host country nationals. American children tend to imitate their parents' behavior toward members of the host society; those whose parents are ethnocentric tend to have the same qualities themselves. In some cases this results in "Ugly Americanism" in the form of condescending attitudes, bad jokes, nasty behavior, and derogatory nicknames. A returnee who lived in Brazil during her teenage years describes the embarrassment she felt at the unwillingness of other Americans to mingle with the Brazilians. "They [the Brazilians] were my hosts," she points out, "and I felt it would insult my host country if I didn't learn their ways."

Some children of Americans overseas are simply homesick. Freelance journalist Claire Kittredge describes them in poignant terms: "One Christmas in Saigon, at age eight, I watched with curiosity as teenage girls across the compound from us made cocoa in the oppressive heat, jitterbugged with one another, and talked wistfully about 'home.' "[2] Most, however, adjust to life between cultures, and many eventually come to prefer an intercultural existence.

A frequent vehicle for participation in the host country culture is the culture itself, especially such elements as music and dance. In Pakistan, for example, American teenagers may study classical Indian dancing or learn to play the sitar. In many posts formal institutions, usually called cultural centers, exist to facilitate cultural exchange. A returnee who spent some of his teenage years in Thailand describes one form of intercultural exchange: "My father was on the board of Mitrapab ("Friendship"), a Thai/American organization that raised funds from parachute jumps to build schools in rural Thailand, from Burma to Malaysia."

Sports clubs and teams and the Boy and Girl Scouts also provide opportunities for intercultural activity. And occasionally American teenagers date host country nationals.

THE PRESENCE OF DANGER

The extent of involvement in the host culture is, naturally, affected by the political situation. For example, one repatriate explains that in Germany in the late 1940s and 1950s "there were still hostile feelings between the Americans and Germans. The American community in Germany tried to maintain as much of an American atmosphere as possible. We had our own clubs, recreational facilities, and housing areas. Socialization with the Germans was limited. Most of the social contact was done by single men with the local German female population. In school we had a German/American Club which met in old bomb bunkers about once a month, but this was not too successful. Most Americans still had hostile feelings toward the German population in general. Those of us in school were taken to a theater and shown about one hour of the confiscated concentration camp films used as evidence in the trials. This did not help us to embrace the German culture or philosophy."

The situation in Vietnam in the mid-1960s is another case in point. As the war escalated, American dependents were limited to

Saigon and two resort areas, and in some families children were discouraged from interacting with Vietnamese children or adults. As a result, they tended to become immersed in the American social round of school, movies, parties, and clubs.

The presence of danger in various forms is something that most Absentee Americans must live with throughout childhood. In the post-World War II years evacuation orders were given to all families upon arrival in Germany: "We all knew where our gathering points were where we would be picked up for evacuation." In the Philippines, American families lived in guarded compounds. Returnees from Third-World countries have been known to comment that their schools had coup days instead of snow days. And the image of Marine machine-gun emplacements on the roof of the American Community School in Saigon is familiar to all who watched television during the mid-1960s; those who attended the school vividly remember the chicken wire stretched over the windows to keep out grenades and the Marine guards on the school buses.

The presence of danger is acknowledged—for example, Foreign Service employees who have been assigned to overseas posts are required to attend a two-day seminar on "Coping with Violence Abroad." Except in extreme circumstances, however, the possibility of incidents such as kidnappings and terrorist acts does not interfere with the day-to-day activities of Absentee Americans. American children living overseas generally feel secure and calm in their home and school environments. In fact, they may express more fear of violence and lawlessness in American cities than of the possibilities of war and terrorism in overseas settings.

LACK OF SUPERVISION

For American teenagers overseas, lack of supervision sometimes creates problems. This is especially true in large communities where adults and teenagers lead parallel lives with little interaction. One returnee who attended high school in Bangkok describes this situation in detail: "In Bangkok, my circle of friends had too much money, too little supervision from parents, too easy access to drugs, alcohol, prostitution, vehicles, and American GIs on R&R from Vietnam—all of whom had six months of war experience, sexual repression, and back pay to let out. We high school students were often happy to show them around and to enjoy their reckless and well-funded behavior with them.

"Bangkok was a place that was exotic, where anything could be bought if only you knew what to ask for, but where we all knew we could never completely fathom the depths of mystery and possibilities for the ultimate psychic, social, or chemical high.

"Something that took years for me to realize was that much of what my circle of friends did overseas was dangerous. Four classmates [out of a high school student body totaling 700] died unnatural deaths. The deaths were due to drug-related suicide, a murder over a drug transaction, a motorcycle wreck, and a drug overdose. We took terrible risks, and any one of us could have suffered the same fate."

The ready availability of cheap marijuana and other drugs (including prescription drugs such as amphetamines and barbiturates) was a particular problem in Bangkok in the late 1960s. But the acting-out behavior of some American teenagers overseas may be a reaction to unusual pressures. One source of pressure is the role of "little ambassador." American children are occasionally told that they, like their parents, represent their country and are expected to behave accordingly. Sponsoring organizations "hold parents responsible for the behavior of their offspring. (If a dependent grossly misbehaves, he or she may be sent home, and the employer may reassign the father or terminate his employment.)"[3] Repatriates from military families often report that they were expected to behave in ways that would reflect favorably on the armed forces in general and their parents' rank in particular; in fact, a DR (delinquency rating) could follow from misbehavior by members of an officer's family. Such requirements create a sense of being constantly under observation that can have long-term consequences, as will become clear later in this book. In the short run, the requirement that a child constantly uphold the honor of his or her family and nation may generate rebellious feelings and behavior.

ECONOMIC PRIVILEGE

No description of life overseas would be complete without some mention of the PX and commissary, shopping facilities available to military and nonmilitary employees of the U.S. government. The PX, or post exchange, is a sort of no-frills department store that stocks items that are in demand among Americans. Usually this means goods brought in from the United States—toiletries, records, and the like—and sold at a discount, but there may be cameras from Germany, electronics from Japan, and other imports, as well as some locally made tourist items. The commissary (described in the *Egypt Post Report* as "similar to a small up-to-date U.S. supermarket") carries American packaged and canned foods and beverages, including such desirables as Twinkies, Butterball turkeys, and fruit roll-ups—visible reminders of the power of the American consumer culture and a source of envy among many host country nationals. Merchandise from the PX and commissary often finds its way onto local black markets, and items like cigarettes and Hershey bars have been used as currency in some areas.

For some families the Sears catalog (and its more recent counterparts) is another important source of consumer goods. Many Absentee Americans can recall the excitement generated by the arrival of Sears orders.

A significant aspect of life overseas is the ready availability of household help. There may be just a maid or an amah, or there may be a complete household staff. In India, for example, "most American families have . . . three to nine servants . . . : a cook, who also does the marketing, a bearer who serves, a person who cleans from the table-tops up, sweepers who clean from the table-tops down, laundryman, nurse, chauffeur, bathroom cleaner, gardener, guard for the grounds. . . . They may live in servants' quarters . . . or they may live in nearby slums."[4]

Absentee Americans often grow up not knowing anything about cooking or housework and not having the habit of doing certain things for themselves. In many countries Americans are expected to hire household help, since it contributes to the local economy, but returnees sometimes have trouble adjusting to servantless homes in the United States, and they may encounter hostility from peers if they mention that they had household help overseas. Some also experience a mild feeling of guilt. "My allowance was the same as the maid's salary," says one repatriate.

On the other hand, a key aspect of life overseas for many Absentee Americans is the opportunity to work in jobs with a service element. Numerous repatriates note that they worked in orphanages, refugee camps, leper clinics, and the like. Others did volunteer work for organizations like Save the Children or provided English-language tutoring for host country children and teenagers.

American children living in Third-World countries are deeply impressed by the disparity between the conditions in which they live and those they see around them. "There is nothing quite like the feeling of being whisked around in an embassy car and seeing tiny hands the size of your own trying to reach through the window at a stop light," writes Kittredge.[5] These experiences have the effect of intensifying the feeling of being highly privileged or blessed that many Absentee Americans report after returning to the United States.

TRANSIENCE

Another prominent aspect of the life of American children overseas is transience: Most move every one, two, or four years. The typical tour of duty is two or three years; tours are sometimes extended, but rarely by more than a year or two. Then the family moves back to the States or to another post, often in the middle of the school year. In addition, a major feature of life overseas for many American families is the furlough or home leave—the occasional return "stateside" for a few weeks. The result of many short tours and furloughs is a constant stream of arrivals and departures at any given post, although it is less visible in the larger overseas communities. The departures often occur at the end of the school year, so that the glee of "no more teachers, no more books" is offset by the sadness of farewell parties and trips to the airport to see off friends whom one is unlikely to meet again.

Transience is a central feature of the nomadic life-style that is characteristic of Absentee Americans, and it has far-reaching consequences. Repeated moves mean the loss of many friends, separation from extended family, and the loss of familiar, comforting places and things, and can give rise to feelings of rootlessness and restlessness.[6] The impact of many moves and changes of environment is reflected in the comments of repatriates throughout this book.

NOTES

1. U.S. Department of State, *Egypt Post Report*, April 1990.

2. Claire Kittredge, "Growing Up Global," *Boston Globe Magazine*, April 3, 1988.

3. Ruth Hill Useem and Richard D. Downie, "Third-Culture Kids," *Today's Education*, September-October 1976, p. 104.

4. Ruth Hill Useem, "The American Family in India," *Annals of the American Academy of Political and Social Sciences*, *368* (1966): 140.

5. Kittredge, "Growing Up Global."

6. Katherine M. Bloomfield, *The Impact of Overseas Living on Adolescent Identity Formation* (Northampton, Mass.: Smith College School for Social Work, 1983).

3

REENTRY

Alas! Whose country have I come to now? Are they some brutal tribe of lawless savages, or a kindly and god-fearing people? Where shall I put all these goods of mine, and where on earth am I myself to go?

— Odysseus

I did not respond at all well to the reentry experience. Though I had spent my entire life thinking I was supposed to belong to this culture, I found I had nothing in common with it. My first two years I did not participate in this culture at all; I didn't know how to and I didn't want to. I couldn't relate to anyone except other foreigners to this country, and no one could relate to me or my experiences.

Reentry. The word connotes reentry into the earth's atmosphere from outer space, and that is an apt description of the experience of reentering the United States after spending much of one's childhood in one or more other countries. The Absentee American returns the way the space shuttle returns, passing through a harsh, hostile atmosphere before coming down to earth.

Tony Karian's experience is entirely typical. Karian was born in Hollywood, California, and lived in the area until the age of nine. During the next eight years his family was stationed in Thailand, Nigeria, and Kenya. When he returned to California at the age of seventeen, he was totally unprepared for the discovery that for him the United States was another foreign country.

Reentry is a significant event for the Absentee American; the experience may be vividly recollected decades later. Respondents described reentry as difficult, painful, turbulent, or traumatic, and they almost universally agreed that the initial period of adjustment—of becoming "acclimated"—lasts from six months to a year or more. The experience is often referred to as a shock; some returnees label it culture shock. In professional literature on the subject, this transition is generally referred to as "reverse culture shock" and is seen as consisting of five phases: initial euphoria, irritability, hostility, gradual adjustment, and adaptation.[1]

The reentry experience is comparable to the experience of the new immigrant—except that the Absentee American is supposedly coming "home" to his or her own culture. And since that culture itself may have changed dramatically during the repatriate's absence, there is sometimes a feeling of disorientation like that experienced by Rip Van Winkle upon waking up from his long sleep, a feeling made even more acute by the vivid "dreams" that the repatriate has had in the interim.

The following comments by an Absentee American who returned to Texas from Germany illustrate the cultural contrasts that characterize the reentry experience: "Living away for over three years may not seem like a long time to someone who's never done it, but it can be a lifetime. *Everything* changes. When I left, girls were not wearing denim jeans. While I was gone, blue jeans really took over—but not in Europe. You can imagine what it was like going to college in 1970 with no blue jeans! I further alienated myself when I wrote a theme in English class dealing with the Vietnam War—only my point of view was in favor of supporting our men who were over there. [In Europe] our TV was a downright joke. We saw 'Gunsmoke,' old horror shows, 'Bonanza' (not current), and Bob Hope's Christmas show—in July. The shows were without commercials, so a one-hour show was forty-five minutes, with fifteen minutes of fillers such as Ruta Lee telling us how and when to mail packages to the States."

THE EXPERIENCE OF MARGINALITY

Long before Absentee Americans began returning "home" in large numbers, Everett Stonequist addressed this issue in a study entitled *The Marginal Man*. "From the moment of his birth," he wrote:

> the human being is the responding subject of a stream of so-cial influences. Before he has learned to speak a single word, or experienced the first glimmer of self-consciousness, he has felt the impress of those activities, standards, and objects which make up that complex whole termed *cul-ture* . . . . Through unconscious as well as conscious in-teraction with other persons he gradually comes to have a recognized place in his particular social world.[2]

But what is that social world? Stonequist was concerned with individuals who "belong" to more than one culture—through mi-gration, education, or marriage—and hence are subject to varying degrees of culture conflict. But the Absentee American belongs to no culture, or perhaps to all cultures. Stonequist's "marginal man" is reproduced endlessly in the Absentee American, who (for the most part) is marginal to the culture or cultures within which he or she grows up, and marginal again to the culture of the United States, regardless of citizenship. As a result, the "social dislocation" experienced by individuals who fall between two racial or cultural groups is magnified in the repatriate.

The experience of moving between cultures can occur, of course, within a nation and can manifest itself in a thousand little ways, such as learning that "regular coffee" isn't the same as "black coffee" and becoming familiar with the local dialect (it's "an arm and a leg," not "a nominal egg"). But when one moves from one nation to another, and especially from a Third-World nation to an urban-industrial one, the experience is magnified many times. Stonequist also commented on this: A person's nationality, he wrote, "forms the widest social environment in which his personality develops." The sense of nationality therefore "is one of the very deeply lodged elements in an individual's self."[3]

The Absentee American often lacks a firmly established national identity, yet upon returning to the United States he or she must function as if such an identity were already fully formed. In reality this is highly unlikely, a fact that is aptly illustrated by the following comment: "I didn't always 'fit in' in Thailand because I was so obviously an American. And yet, when you return to the States, you're so obviously 'un-American' because you haven't grown up here. When you first return, you're caught between two cultures." Another returnee echoes this thought: "By the time I graduated at eighteen from Nairobi International School only four of my years had been spent in the United States. I had an identity crisis; I knew I was not African and yet I knew little of the culture that I was supposedly a member of."

The vast majority of repatriates say that for the first few months after returning to the United States they felt out of touch with American culture because they had little in common with peers who had not lived abroad. As one returnee puts it, "I felt like I was not really a part of the U.S. cultural scene; people did not really know how to deal with me." Others put it more simply: "I felt like a stranger in a strange land"; "I was a fish out of water"; "I may as well have been on the moon [or 'from the moon']." Even those who had little difficulty adjusting to life in the United States note that they were "out of step" in terms of clothes, language, and the like.

The cultural differences that make the returnee an "alien" take a variety of forms. Two teenage returnees from the Middle East report that they needed to learn the following: how to use a Metro fare card machine; that building addresses are odd numbers on one side of the street and even on the other; what the "call waiting" signal on the telephone sounds like; what a "snow day" is; who Oprah Winfrey is; what *Cliff Notes* are; how to get a telephone number from Information; who the Pet Shop Boys are; what an ATM is; and more.[4] But the array of cultural matters that are unfamiliar to the repatriate may include a great deal more. For example, there is the matter of driving: Many Absentee Americans do not have a license and are not used to traveling by car; nor do they know anything about cars, or care. There is the matter of shopping, of being able to buy almost anything one wants after living in places where many consumer goods were not available. There are unfamiliar things to operate, ranging from water fountains to garbage disposers. There are the mores of teen society—especially those governing relations with the opposite sex. There are supermarkets, shopping malls, fast food, cruising, drugs. There are slang phrases and in-jokes. Everyday life is very different: From the returnee's viewpoint, everyone seems to be in a hurry; the pace of life is frighteningly fast. And there is that pervasive pride in all things American; the mere suggestion that anything about another culture might be superior (or even acceptable) has earned many returnees the label "communist."

From the standpoint of the repatriate, the United States is a very demanding society. Americans are expected to know a great deal, to be able to converse about politics, sports, movies and television, celebrities of all kinds. They are expected to want to get places fast, preferably by car. They are supposed to know how to shop—especially for clothing—and to devote considerable time and attention to this activity. They are expected not only to know how to compete but to *want* to compete—in business, sports, and other pursuits. Returnees who did not grow up in such an environment find themselves culturally adrift. As David Pollock explains, "Knowing a culture is a little like 'Trivial Pursuit.' You don't study it, you live through it. You collect lots of information—values, bits and pieces of history, the names of athletes, in-jokes, humor, code words—and store it away. Then, during personal exchanges, you dip back into the data bank and pull them out and make connections with other people." Returnees lack the appropriate "data bank."[5] In addition, the people around them often are totally uninterested in their experiences or, worse, believe them to be showing off or "snotty" if they mention having lived in another country.

It is very difficult for people (especially children) who have not lived overseas to relate to returnees. At best, returnees are viewed as a novelty; they may be asked to say something in a foreign language or to give a classroom talk on the country they have just left. Sometimes a returnee is viewed as a fascinating mystery: "I even had kids run up and touch me, then run away!" In almost all cases the returnee is viewed as an oddity in the United States. Indeed, the phrase "I was an oddity" is echoed over and over again by returnees. "It felt weird," says one. "My friends really didn't know what to say to me." Says another, "I felt very different. Other people viewed me as an odd person." A third remarks, "I might as well have had antennas the way a lot of people reacted. The minute some people found out I grew up overseas I became an alien from another planet!"

OUTSIDERS IN SCHOOL

Absentee Americans face a variety of difficulties in their efforts to find a place for themselves among their peers. Some enter elementary school and face the careless taunts of schoolmates—"the kids made fun of me because I talked about Santiago and I told them there was no such thing as Sesame Street." In the elementary school years the main problem is that the other children have already established their social order and peer groups, so the returnee is by definition an outsider. In the later school years the problem becomes more complex. High school students have a particularly difficult time since their experiences are totally different from those of the typical American teenager. Carol Naughton, who spent most of her high school years in Pakistan, says, "Reentry was a terrible experience for me. I returned to a school in my senior year with kids I had grown up with through grade school. Suddenly we had nothing in common and I was treated as an outsider." Another repatriate says, "I was quite miserable. I entered a huge American high school in my last year. I shared neither the cultural nor the intellectual values of my peers."

Besides encountering firmly established cliques, the returnee may find that philosophical differences stand in the way of acceptance by peers. This is a frequent experience for Absentee Americans from military families. "I was hurt and insulted," says one. "I had a very strong allegiance to my country. Therefore, I was very surprised and quite shocked to learn, for the first time, that many Americans have little understanding of the military experience." The outcome in such cases tends to be greater dedication to schoolwork coupled with lack of interest in social activities.

Many returnees enter more rigidly structured schools with much larger classes than are typically found in overseas schools, especially high schools. Teenagers who were accustomed to a school with perhaps eighty students may suddenly find themselves in one with 1,500 or 2,000 students. Moreover, they may have to shift from one-teacher classrooms to a system in which students move from class to class throughout the school day. And in many overseas schools the faculty members and parents are much more involved in the operation of the school and in providing counseling and support for the students than is typical in a public school in the United States.

"Army brats" constitute a special case: They must adjust to civilian schools as well as to life in the typical American elementary or high school. One former army brat says, "The civilians were not sure how to handle us or our experiences. Maybe they were afraid to get close to us because they knew we were there temporarily." On the other hand, living on a college campus is somewhat like living on a military base, making it easier for the army brat to adjust to college than to high school.

ANOTHER FOREIGN COUNTRY

American society at large is also strange to returnees, who often describe it as if it were a totally alien culture. For example: "I found Americans provincial and unsophisticated about the world but very advanced sexually and materialistically." "Americans ostentatiously displayed their wealth. The hugeness of the country and the speed on the freeways was frightening." "I found the Americans very friendly but I was overwhelmed by the enormity of the shopping centers, schools, supermarkets, etc."

Some repatriates say that they experienced "entry" rather than "reentry." To them the United States was another foreign country with a new culture to be learned and adjusted to, including learning how to use the currency, "learning" American-English (i.e., slang and idioms), finding out how to shop for everyday items, and so forth. Repatriates for whom reentry was more like entry for the first time tend to emphasize the emotional shock of the experience. As one returnee puts it, "It was damn near the hardest thing I've ever done. Others responded [negatively], which led to alienation and anger on my part. As a result, most of my friends were foreigners—whom I can associate with more comfortably." Another notes that her friends were people "who were still discovering themselves, still plagued by doubts. . . . They didn't fit the normal pattern."

Rebecca Sholes, an Absentee American who spent the majority of her childhood years in India, exemplifies these repatriates. "For all intents and purposes," she says, "my experience was very much that of a foreign student. Though I looked American and sounded American, my values and perspective on life were not purely American. I did not feel comfortable until I got involved with the foreign student community, particularly the Indian students, and began to seek out courses on South Asia. This gave me a cultural reference point and helped me to feel connected to the past."

Absentee Americans often feel more alien upon returning to the United States than they did upon arriving in a supposedly foreign

country. Indeed, those who have been most successful in adapting
to a host culture usually have the most difficulty adjusting to their
"homeland."[6] Many returnees report that they felt like foreigners
and even were mistaken for foreigners at times: "Until I moved
to the U.S. I always thought I was American—that is how my
Brazilian friends saw me. After I arrived, my American friends
saw me as a Brazilian." The feeling of being caught between
two cultures may explain why returnees tend to make friends
with people from a foreign or international background, or from
a different ethnic group, who are better able to understand "where
they are coming from."

"WHERE ARE YOU FROM?"

An immense problem for returnees is the question "Where are
you from?" This question is asked with great frequency. One
Absentee American who has returned to the United States several
times points out that "it's hard for others to not have a place where
you're from to help them put you in context." Yet there seems
to be no way for an Absentee American to answer the question
without eliciting reactions ranging from doubt to incredulity to
disdain. Although most people profess to be interested in life
in other countries, the feeling that repatriates are showing off
often results in stressful interactions. The following comment
is typical: "I soon found that others were not interested in the
'unusual' or thought if I wasn't boasting then I certainly had to
be exaggerating." Even if the returnee is not viewed as a snob,
he or she may be treated as an oddity "from nowhere."

Rebecca Sholes describes such an experience: "I really felt
cut off from my international background and found it hard
to relate to the people around me who had grown up in the
United States. When people talked about their hometown, if I
shared my experiences growing up in South Asia they could
not relate as I could not relate to their experiences. Often if I
discussed the places I had traveled to, the things I had done, I

got the feeling that people thought I was a snob and was trying to show off."

Eventually the repatriate is likely to clam up to avoid further psychological punishment. One returnee says, "After being told I was very tall for an Oriental (when I returned from Korea), I stopped mentioning I had ever been abroad." Another adds, "We learned not to ever talk about our past so that the experience of living overseas would not come up. You can only deny living with Tarzan and the apes so many times." Similar experiences are reported by almost all repatriates. Diane Anderson, for example, recounts an incident that occurred at a liberal midwestern college: "A blind date asked me where I was from. I said, 'Karachi, Pakistan,' and heard him turn to another man with us and say, mockingly, 'Karachi, *Pah-kee-stahn!*' From then on, I said I was from Missoula, Montana."

To the Absentee American, saying "When I lived in Karachi . . . " is no different from saying "When I lived in Chicago . . . ," but the perceptions of others do not permit the repatriate to indulge in such recollections. Sooner or later most returnees learn strategies to avoid naming places, such as saying "I grew up in the Foreign Service" or "I was an army brat." Or they brush the question aside—"I'm from New Jersey, how about you?" This learning process can be painful, however, since in effect it means repudiating part of one's self.

A few repatriates, resenting others' perception of them as strange, react by rejecting American culture entirely and becoming loners, often creating a private world centering on studies or hobbies. One repatriate comments, "I found Americans extremely cold and insensitive; I withdrew from a culture I found intimidating and was perceived as arrogant and reserved."

ISSUES OF STATUS

Another source of problems for returnees is the change in status that accompanies the change in cultural context. In some countries (fewer today than in the 1940s and 1950s) Americans are highly regarded, and in many places American families are extremely well off relative to the local population and can obtain high-quality housing and a large household staff. But upon returning to the United States the Absentee American becomes "just like everyone else" in terms of housing, schooling, dress, and other aspects of social status, a change that requires a myriad of adjustments that can be as mundane as learning to make one's own bed or as subtle as learning that one should not address one's parents' friends by their first names. Many have to learn how to cook and clean—"I hardly knew what a vacuum cleaner was!" is a typical comment. Here again there is great potential for misunderstanding. One Absentee American who returned to Maryland and attended a suburban elementary school mentioned that there had been servants in his family's house overseas. Soon his schoolmates were spreading the rumor that the family had owned slaves.

Not only do repatriates encounter issues of status, but they must adjust to the attitudes and prejudices of others. A returnee from Morocco relates how she was the first to arrive in her shared dorm room at college. "I dropped off my bag and went on to explore the campus," she says. "I later found out that my roommate's mother had spotted the 'Morocco' sticker on my suitcase and threatened to take her daughter right back home if she had been assigned a room with an 'African.' " Another repatriate reports that she did not appreciate the racial problems in the United States until she was in Georgia in 1965 and was told that she was drinking from the "black" water fountain.

THE NEED FOR SOCIAL ANCHORAGE

Another factor affecting the emotional adjustment of returnees is homesickness. Again and again they mention that they did not want to return and were homesick for the places they had left; some also missed close friends and family members who remained overseas. Many felt depressed for several months after returning. As Ruth Van Reken writes in *Letters Never Sent*, "It's

sort of like death—to lose your whole world in one moment."
Indeed, during their childhood years Absentee Americans may
experience a great deal of grief at the loss of friends and familiar surroundings. That grief is often unexpressed, yet it can
have lasting effects on the returnee's personality, a fact that is
discussed in numerous books and articles on the psychology of
the "third-culture kid." It is theorized that the grief caused by
a series of partings, if unexpressed and unresolved, may lead
to deep-seated anger or depression. (In addition, as a result of
jet travel, the transition between countries occurs much more
rapidly than in the past, often within a few hours and following a
rushed farewell period; this prevents closure, or the psychological
separation of one stage of life from the next.) The experience of
frequent partings may also make the returnee hesitant to form
close relationships for fear of being hurt again.[7]

Returnees who are able to become members of a group with
shared goals, such as a sports team, gain immediate access to
friends and group acceptance. This goes a long way toward allevi-
ating the emotional pain they may experience during reentry. In a
novel entitled *The Marginal Man* (which makes explicit reference
to Stonequist's work), L. C. Tsung makes this point in describing
the experience of Chinese residents of the United States:

> We are now transplanted into a new culture, vigorous and
> pragmatic, possessing a set of values and emphases to which
> we are not accustomed but which we are obliged to accept.
> We are moving along the margin of each culture, so to
> speak, with every word we speak and every act we perform.
> We are constantly touching the borders of both cultures,
> whether we like it or not.

Tsung notes that this dilemma is bound to create insecurity, and
that the solution is to seek social anchorage. "Threatened with insecurity, the Marginal Man seeks social anchorage through membership in some sort of group, whether it be a political party, a
religious creed, or a clan guild."

Social anchorage is what the Absentee American lacks, and desperately needs. The time required to find such an anchorage varies considerably and in some cases extends over a lifetime.

Some returnees say that reentry was not a problem for them. Upon close examination, however, it turns out that many of them had visited the United States at frequent intervals and returned to the homes and neighborhoods in which they had spent their early childhood. They had maintained friendships from those years and were able to reestablish those ties upon returning. But even in these cases there may be problems. Priscilla Ervin, who returned to Texas from Japan just before entering the seventh grade, explains: "We lived in the same house as before, so I was going to school with the same kids I had known in third and fourth grade. [But] I could not pick it up again. The same girls I had been friends with were all still friends, but they just weren't interested. There's something about having lived overseas. I now think the problem lies with the other people, not me. I certainly didn't have this figured out at age thirteen, however!"

For some repatriates the experience of moving from one culture to another during childhood comes in handy when they return to the States. For them, reentry may be difficult, but is no worse than adjusting to other cultures. This attitude occurs most often among Absentee Americans who spent their childhood years in a variety of countries or whose families alternated between tours of duty overseas and "stateside." They often comment that their varied experiences made it easy for them to talk to strangers, and that the latter responded to them positively. And for returnees who came back under dramatic circumstances, such as the evacuation of American dependents from Vietnam in February 1965, reentry was generally a positive experience, since their peers tended to view them as quasi-heroes and asked them numerous questions out of genuine curiosity.

There is also a small group of returnees who seem to have been largely insulated from the cultures of the countries in which their families were stationed—who attended American schools with other American children, shopped at the American PX, went to the American-run library, attended American movies, and so on. As one returnee comments, "Having lived in an American community while in Japan and Germany I always felt American and at times it was hard to remember that I was actually living in a foreign country." These repatriates speak of coming "home" to "the land of the Big PX," or say that returning to the United States was like going to Disneyland. (They may also call the United States "the land of the round doorknob"; doors in European countries have handles; those in Oriental countries lack doorknobs.) They sometimes comment, however, that they found the countries they visited interesting and that they had wonderful adventures. Their perspective is more similar to that of the tourist than to that of the resident.

A returnee who has a positive view of reentry is Mark Julian, whose father, an army officer, was stationed at numerous bases both in the United States and abroad. For Julian, returning to the United States from the Philippines, and later from Germany, was a new adventure. "I looked forward to these moves because I liked to have new ways of doing things, seeing what I put in storage so long ago, new people, places, and things." He points out that when he was overseas he "had most of what Americans had—*Stars and Stripes* [the English-language newspaper of the armed forces], library, movies, TV, cars, houses, hospitals, radio." "What I like best," he remarks, "is that I had two cultures available to mix and match the best." He adds: "I accept change and use it as positively as possible."

Another repatriate comments: "At eighteen years old I felt very special. Others thought I was very lucky to have had such an experience at such an early age." All that was necessary for a successful reentry, for this returnee and others with a similar outlook, was to become reacquainted with hamburgers and fries, catch up on the latest dances, and find out what was new on TV. "The first thing I did when I got through customs was to eat a 'real' hamburger at the snack bar in the terminal," says one. Many comment on being able to rely on the availability of favorite foods such as Cheerios and Jello. As one returnee comments, "When we returned to the States I was amazed at how wonderful America was! I was overwhelmed by just about everything: my first Hires Root Beer in Miami's airport, eating five American candy bars at one time, . . . "

At the other extreme are repatriates who have grown up almost entirely in another culture. This is most likely to occur among missionary families. Often the children live in Third-World countries, perhaps attending boarding schools, and do not return to the United States until the age of seventeen or eighteen. For them, reentry may be especially traumatic, even though on the surface they may appear to adapt. In the words of Howard Bearsdlee, who grew up in Mali and attended boarding school in Guinea, "I decided that life was not predictable or coherent, and that to survive you need to quickly adjust to anything that comes along. It's as if you develop a tremendous 'clutch' in your psyche which allows you to shift gears whenever necessary."

An important force motivating the returnee to adapt is the desire for acceptance by peers; this may be the key determinant in the degree to which reentry is remembered as a positive or negative experience. Many report that they worked hard at "fitting in" by becoming culturally literate: studying the teen culture, listening attentively to popular music, wearing "cool" clothes, and the like. As one returnee describes it, "I never fully identified myself with the U.S., but went through much anxiety and effort to try to 'fit in'—to feel I belonged and was accepted." "American teenagers were beyond me," says another. "I spent my first years trying to catch up, figuring out who the Grateful Dead were and the proper degree of nonchalance."

This process of gaining acceptance results in a compromise between the self and the expectations of others. As Stonequist explains, "The individual's self is an integral part of his social role, and when this social role is fundamentally changed the individual's self is forced through a similar transformation."[8] Beth Rambo, the daughter of a medical missionary who spent many years in Zaire, sums up this experience as follows: "When I came back to go to college after four years of high school in Kinshasa,

I felt very different, yet I wanted to be accepted, not singled out, so I felt a strange combination of apologetic and defiant about my Zairean experience. People did accept me, but that whole part of my life, which they seemed unable to comprehend, was rarely acknowledged." Rambo, like most returnees, had to give up part of her former self in the process of acquiring a new and more stable identity.

NOTES

1. Kay Branaman Eakin, *The Foreign Service Teenager—At Home in the U.S.: A Few Thoughts for Parents Returning with Teenagers* (Washington, D.C.: Overseas Briefing Center, Foreign Service Institute, U.S. Department of State, May 1988).

2. Everett Stonequist, *The Marginal Man: A Study in Personality and Culture Conflict* (New York: Russell and Russell, 1937), p. 1.

3. Stonequist, *The Marginal Man*, p. 7.

4. Eakin, *The Foreign Service Teenager—At Home in the U.S.*

5. David C. Pollock, quoted in Claire Kittredge, "Growing Up Global," *Boston Globe Magazine*, April 3, 1988.

6. Tom J. Lewis and Robert E. Jungman, eds., *On Being Foreign: Culture Shock in Short Fiction* (Yarmouth, Maine: Intercultural Press, 1986).

7. Eakin, *The Foreign Service Teenager—At Home in the U.S.*

8. Stonequist, *The Marginal Man*, p. 6.

4

FITTING IN

The adaptation of the newcomer to the in-group which at first seemed to be strange and unfamiliar to him is a continuous process of inquiry into the cultural pattern of the approached group. If this process of inquiry succeeds, then this pattern and its elements will become to the newcomer a matter of course, an unquestionable way of life, a shelter, and a protection.

—Alfred Schutz

For people raised in the United States, "being an American" is likely to be taken for granted. For anyone who travels abroad on a vacation or business trip, it is a matter of carrying a U.S. passport. But for those who live overseas for an extended period with the intent of returning, being an American is a matter of identity that goes far beyond citizenship. The label "American" brings special treatment—not always positive, but special nonetheless.

The "American" label creates an identity independent of the individual bearing the label, an identity so strong that some may try to shed it, either temporarily or permanently. One returnee tells how she tried to shed the label during a bus tour of Paris with a multicultural group that included many Americans. She spoke French with a Swiss accent and said that she was Swiss.

For Americans stationed abroad, the status of American citizen is all-encompassing. It becomes what sociologists call a master status. Almost all aspects of day-to-day life are related to that status. One may have special housing, often with a complete household staff; one's car may have diplomatic plates; one's children may attend American or "international" schools where they are taught in English. In some overseas posts there are American clubs and community centers that show imported movies and attempt to duplicate American fast food. For shopping, there are the PX and the commissary.

These outward manifestations of American-ness are, of course, much less significant than the internal effects of this master status. One is enshrouded in American-ness; all of one's relationships, not only with other Americans but with members of the host culture, are colored by the fact of citizenship. This one identity subsumes all others, so that gender, race, religion, education, or any other characteristic becomes almost irrelevant.

This is not to say that Absentee Americans walk around like automatons or little wind-up American dolls. They are individuals in Athens and Bangkok just as they are in Chicago and San Francisco. But they are *American* individuals, and the reflections they see in the eyes of others are the images of American citizens living overseas.

With citizenship constituting such a large portion of a person's identity overseas, what happens when that person returns to the United States and finds citizenship taken for granted and largely irrelevant to day-to-day existence? The Absentee American is not used to being just like everyone else. The lack of self-definition as an American in a foreign setting leaves what might be described as an identity gap, a space that is not immediately filled by a sense of local citizenship in a place that may be as strange to the returnee as any foreign nation encountered for the first time.

Many Absentee Americans take a long time to become integrated into American society. Even twenty or more years later, the returnee is likely to express ambivalence about his or her nationality and place in American society. Typical is Anthony Bates, who spent his childhood in London, Paris, Hong Kong, and West Berlin. "I am equally at home and equally foreign in the United Kingdom and the United States," he says; he goes on to describe himself as "a misfit and also the fortunate possessor of two 'homes.' " In fact, many respondents use the word *home* to refer to the country in which they grew up; this is most common among Absentee Americans who spent many years in a single country, as is frequently true of missionary families. One repatriate from such a family comments: "Outwardly, I'm white and speak 'regular' English; the African part of me doesn't show and periodically re-emerges in my dreams. I miss Africa."

CULTURAL CHAMELEONS?

Some repatriates express the belief that they will never be well integrated into any society. Having been required to adapt to many environments throughout childhood, they feel that they can find a niche wherever they go. In fact, they pride themselves on their adaptability; the image of a chameleon comes up often, coupled with reluctance to commit oneself to any particular environment. (As Graham Greene described it in *The Comedians*, "transience was my pigmentation.") Martha Opdahl is typical. Between 1940 and 1958 her family moved more than ten times. "I adapt easily to whatever the situation is—I am a chameleon in a sense—but I maintain my values and principles. I feel comfortable living in the United States. I know its ways. But I feel totally alienated when I see socially sanctioned prejudice—sexual, racial and ethnic."

This widely shared outlook may explain the tendency of repatriates to settle in places whose populations are highly diverse. Thus, Marcia Welles, who grew up in Colombia, Chile, Cuba, Pakistan, and South Africa, says, "I think New York may be the only place I could live—it's multi-national, multi-racial, multi-everything." Another returnee adds, "New York City is a rather ideal place to live for a person who's combined American and international backgrounds. You can hear every language spoken, eat in restaurants from every conceivable country, purchase goods from every corner of the globe. The city, in its current role of economic and cultural 'world capital,' also acts as a magnet to old friends from all over the globe."

Washington is another popular location; its inhabitants are described as accepting and open-minded. Another desirable feature of Washington from the returnee's perspective is the transience of much of its population. According to Beth Shearer, who grew up in a Foreign Service family, "Washington is a very transient place so I am not at a disadvantage. I don't think I would have integrated well into a small, stable community."

This is not to say that reintegration is an unattainable goal. Some repatriates comment that after recovering from the shock of reentry they made a conscious effort to become accepted and to establish a place for themselves, often beginning with their work environment. Most, however, continue to feel like outsiders. Their experience suggests that the feeling of being an outsider becomes ingrained in the Absentee American's personality as a result of living "on the outside" for several years during childhood and adolescence.

One way of dealing with the feeling of being an outsider is to keep moving. Many repatriates gravitate toward jobs that require them to travel to various regions of the nation, if not the world, and to explore different regional cultures. Another strategy is to find a particular niche or specialized environment—often occupational—and concentrate on it. One returnee comments: "I've adjusted only in the sense that I'm basically at peace with myself and my work; but without my work I would have to journey abroad to find release."

The integration process may be intertwined with the process of searching for roots. It can be seen as part of the "Where are you from?" syndrome. Chuck Tigue, who describes himself as an "air force brat," sums up the situation as follows: "There was a sense of not-belonging while I was growing up. When people asked where I was from I had to say, 'What year?' Now I have put down roots and I can say that I am from Oklahoma City. I feel like I belong here. It is that belonging that makes me feel well integrated into American society." Another returnee says, "All the moving caused me to seek a small community where I'd belong, know people for more than a few years, and life would be stable."

Repatriates often remark that becoming reintegrated into American society is a long, slow process. It takes time to understand and appreciate the values of Americans who have never lived outside the United States. If those values remain "foreign," the feeling of being an outsider will persist for many years. Diane Terry, who lived in Kenya for most of her childhood, is typical. "Now, I am [integrated]," she says, "but for the first few years, I felt like a fish out of water. I was much too trusting of people and much too naive." Another returnee adds: "It took years to figure out how society *worked*. I didn't catch on to social procedures easily." Other returnees say that they feel well integrated now, "but it was a struggle."

Many returnees also point out that it is difficult to become part of a small community when one has not grown up there—another reason for favoring larger cities. Even after more than forty years repatriates may feel that the integration process is not complete. They feel that they have very little in common with people who have lived in the same town or state all their lives. They are likely to have friends who have lived in other states, if not other countries, and they tend to be more interested in history, geography, and world affairs than other members of their communities. As one returnee comments, "I would say that I am better integrated into American society now than when I first came because I have a better understanding of the people, the culture, and how the system works. However, I still move very much in an international context, without which I feel like a fish out of water. All my jobs have involved working with international people and global issues, and my friends are primarily people who have a foot in two worlds. I still carry a sense of foreignness with me."

A few repatriates express no doubt at all about fitting in. They report that they are "absolutely integrated. Why not?" Or they say that they "fit in as well as anyone." They note that from their earliest years they have learned how to adapt to different cultures and societies, so adapting to American society was relatively easy. Some feel that they are more politically aware and more patriotic as a result of their overseas experiences. Their attitudes toward the United States tend to be very positive, and they call it "home."

As might be expected, Absentee Americans who were not absent very long are more likely to feel that they are well integrated into American society. Even they, however, point out that they feel at home in other countries as well as in the United States. They note, too, that the process of becoming integrated is hard work and that the support of friends and family is important. One returnee notes that she had a close friend and "cultural guide" throughout college who eased the adjustment process.

A BASIC DICHOTOMY

There are indications that repatriates may become integrated into American society on one level but not on others. Michael Karian, who spent his childhood in Thailand, Nigeria, and Kenya, reports that he feels well integrated on a surface level, "but deeper, more emotionally, no! I still feel different and plan on traveling/working overseas when possible. I consider life here temporary till I find my 'niche' in the world—if I ever do!" Like Karian, many Absentee Americans distinguish between "levels" of integration. The following comment is typical: "On the surface, I feel as though I am well integrated into American society, but on another level I feel as though I am from outer space."

For social scientists, the duality expressed by repatriates comes as no surprise. As Everett Stonequist wrote, "If the cultural differences are of major importance, [the marginal man's] dual social connections will . . . be reflected in the type of life he leads, the nature of his achievements or failures, his conception of himself, and many of his social attitudes and aspirations. He will, in fact, be a kind of dual personality."[1]

This dichotomy is often expressed in remarks that indicate ambivalence toward American society. "I have followed the social norm," says Russell Fritz, who lived in Pakistan between the ages of thirteen and seventeen; "that is, I have credit cards, mortgages, and the material possessions which indicate social integration. But I feel alienated from, and concerned by, our foreign policy or lack thereof." Muriel Smith, who lived in India in her late teens, sums up the matter by stating that integration "depends on whether you're talking about functional integration or full-blown personal identification with society." Most returnees could be described as functionally integrated but do not identify personally with American society. As one returnee puts it, "I can pass as a mainstream American although I very much resist being perceived as one."

In some cases ambivalence about fitting into American society may stem from a feeling that complete integration is not necessary. As one returnee remarks, "I am as well integrated into this society as I ever will be. To me this is just another culture to master and I have mastered it as well as I want to. I know how to behave and what to say as well as or better than most Americans, but I don't consider myself a part of this society per se. I don't harbor any particular animosity toward this culture, but I am clearly aware of its limitations."

There are also some returnees who are determined not to become reintegrated into American society because of a lack of respect for the United States and all that it represents. They constitute a small minority, however.

Returnees often point out that there is a difference between behaviors and attitudes; Absentee Americans may eventually learn appropriate behaviors and social norms, but their opinions and beliefs may differ considerably from those of the majority of the population. A repatriate who lived in England and Pakistan for part of her childhood says, "I know now how to follow form and play the game but not from any real belief or allegiance. I have never felt integrated into any society as an adult; I am merely an observer. I still find no comprehension of my perspective from *anyone* except fellow repatriates." Even returnees who identify themselves as "loyal patriots" say that they occasionally become angry at what they perceive as misguided foreign policy.

It appears that for the majority of returnees integration into American society is incomplete, if it occurs at all. They may say, for example, that they "have adjusted as much as possible." This feeling is expressed by Sherry Tousley, the daughter of an army officer who moved thirteen times during her childhood: "I generally know how to function in U.S. society but I seem to prefer other countries, products made outside the United States. I get excited over exposure to other countries to a far greater extent than over exposure to U.S. culture. I long to live abroad again!" Another returnee expresses the same thought more simply: "My heart is in Europe. I gravitate toward things in the States that remind me of Europe." An Absentee American who grew up in Mexico says, "Although I am now comfortable with [American society], I prefer the values and mores of Mexico. I am still very homesick."

Even repatriates who have overcome their homesickness for things foreign seem unable to complete the transition to things American. They tend to feel that fads come and go so fast that it's impossible to keep up with them. In the words of one returnee, "There are times, still, when I feel out of place simply because I never caught up to the American trendy style of clothes, nor did I pick up on new slang." Years later returnees may find themselves "drawing a blank" at words or expressions that are familiar to others around them. Some returnees also find that it is difficult to know how to dress appropriately for different work situations or social occasions. One repatriate says, "The biggest problem is that sometimes I find there are gaps in my American cultural experience from the years I was away." Another notes, "I missed out on all the cultural landmarks of my generation—[for example,] I never watched the 'Howdy Doody Show.' "

An Absentee American who spent her childhood in Brazil says that she has felt "somewhat handicapped" since returning to the United States. "I have experienced too much cross-cultural confusion," she says. "It has taken me too long to 'learn the ropes'!" As a result, "I've had a very difficult time defining myself over the years." This reaction is typical of individuals who identify with the standards of two or more social groups: The conflict may be experienced as an acute personal difficulty or mental tension.[2]

A FEELING OF DIFFERENTNESS

Absentee Americans are constantly aware of aspects of their childhoods that are unlike those of contemporaries who were raised in the United States. Repatriates' recollections of life overseas often have an epic quality. Childhood memories are mused over, polished in the mind until they glow, strung together like Christmas lights. Returnees may take mental refuge in a sort of never-never land of overseas events, places, and life-styles. This is the environment they grew up in, the one in which they feel most at home. This feeling can have some unanticipated consequences. One returnee reports: "I had a very strong reaction when the North Vietnamese changed the name of Saigon to Ho Chi Minh City. It felt as if a part of my childhood had slipped into a black hole, and that I was having to work hard to keep from following it."

The feeling of being different from other Americans is a central factor in the Absentee American's adjustment to life in the United States. A repatriate who spent her childhood in India comments: "I've never stopped feeling different. Different things shaped my life, different things matter to me, friends' nostalgia trips leave me out." The reentry experience may be painful precisely because of this differentness; however, as time goes by returnees tend to become more comfortable with this feeling and in some cases to cherish it and seek ways to employ it constructively. As one returnee says, "I've always been outside 'normal' American life, and creatively, intellectually, and spiritually, I feel that's just fine."

To some extent, the process of adjusting to American life may be viewed as one of gaining cultural literacy. As E. D. Hirsch, Jr., explains,

Although it is true that no two humans know exactly the same things, they often have a great deal of knowledge in common. To a large extent this common knowledge or collective memory allows people to communicate, to work together, and to live together. It forms the basis for communities, and . . . it is a distinguishing characteristic of a national culture.[3]

In this connection, it is instructive to note that the subtitle of Hirsch's *Dictionary of Cultural Literacy* is "What Every American Needs to Know."

As the repatriate becomes increasingly "literate" in American culture, filling in the blanks left empty by childhood absence, he or she becomes more and more comfortable with life in American society.

MILITARY BRATS AND MISSIONARY KIDS

Repatriates from a military background can be viewed as a special category. Having spent much of their childhood in military communities, they have had to adjust to civilian life as well as to life in American society. But they have reacted in two quite different ways. Some feel well integrated into American society and often express surprise at the idea that they might not feel that way. For them, the military environment seems to have provided a stable set of values that compensated for their geographic mobility. Typical is Mary Jean Stump, who comments: "Yes, of course I [feel well integrated]. After all, I had been going to American schools, with Americans, and had access to American

PXs, libraries, and snack bars." Another returnee adds, "I feel that military brats are generally better adjusted as adults than our peers are. We are required at an early age to adjust to constantly changing environments. We learn early to meet people, jump into new cultures, and take risks." (In her case the need to adjust applied not only to the cultures of Germany and Okinawa but also to those of Missouri, Kansas, Washington, Idaho, California, Texas, Virginia, Georgia, and Illinois.)

Other self-styled "military brats" had difficulty adjusting to the civilian culture and found that adjustment to American society was a trivial matter by comparison. One notes that membership in the military community provides a solid network and a superimposed identity that is greatly missed after returning to the United States and civilian life. Another says that in the military "there was no such thing as a stranger because everyone was a stranger." Even twenty years after returning to the United States, these repatriates may feel out of place in civilian society and miss the military life. Priscilla Ervin, daughter of a fighter pilot, says that she feels "pretty well integrated" and "totally civilianized" twenty years after returning to the United States, yet "a part of me still feels different."

A similar split appears among repatriates from missionary families. Some feel that they are fully integrated into the Christian community wherever they happen to be. Others say that the main problem for them upon returning to the United States was to adjust to life outside the church, and that becoming reintegrated into American society was much less traumatic. They may share the sentiments of Marian Adams, who was born in Batang (Tibet) of missionary parents: "I felt I was an alien, that there was something inherently wrong with me, and that there was no way to change my aloneness."

Dr. Clyde Austin of Abilene Christian University has devoted considerable study to reentry in general and missionary families in particular. He has identified several factors that influence the missionary kid's experience of reentry and reintegration. In contrast to most American families overseas, missionary families are not officially sponsored, are more dependent on the local economy, stay overseas longer, may be geographically isolated, and are more likely to send their children to local schools or boarding schools. Missionary families are also more likely to develop a sense of divided loyalty between the host country and the home country. Thus, while the missionary family may be better prepared for life in another culture, missionary kids are often less well prepared for life in the United States.[4]

INCOMPLETE REINTEGRATION

The problems associated with reintegration are complex; few Absentee Americans can give an equivocal "yes" or "no" answer to the question of whether they are well integrated into American society. Their confusion is illustrated in the following response by a returnee who has not yet resolved the issue: "I still can't communicate with people. How far can a conversation go when you can't refer to the previous events in life—the travel or the experiences? Some unbelievable experiences pass through my mind as I'm standing in line at the supermarket realizing that I could not relate them to anyone I might meet in this town without sounding boastful."

Not feeling free to talk about the foreign places in which they have lived is a continual problem for Absentee Americans. Indeed, one returnee identifies this as the central issue of reintegration: "I feel that with time I finally integrated myself into American society by subjugating my desire to talk about Europe." This issue is illustrated by the comments of an Absentee American who returned to New Jersey at the age of eighteen and found a job in a grocery store: "After learning I was from out of state, they asked me what I was. I had no rational response; overseas the answer was a definite 'I am an American' so I tried that. By their laughter and the look on their faces I knew this was not what they were asking. So I tried again: 'I was born here in New Jersey.' Now they thought I was dumb, or had something to hide."

One explanation for this feeling of being in a sort of cultural limbo is provided by E. D. Hirsch, Jr., in his well-known works on cultural literacy. We take for granted, Hirsch notes, "that one literate person knows approximately the same things as another and is aware of the probable limits of the other person's knowledge. . . . In order to speak effectively to people we must have a reliable sense of what they do and do not know."[5] The constraints imposed by this situation are summarized in the following quite typical comment: "There is a huge part of my life I can't share with anyone unless it is someone else who was raised in foreign countries."

It is this quality of Absentee Americans (and citizens of other nations who have had similar experiences) that has led sociologists and psychologists to identify repatriates as a "third culture," one whose roots may be found neither in American society nor in the host countries in which they have lived, but in the shared background and experiences of repatriates themselves. Members of this third culture often have more in common with one another than with Americans who were raised in the United States. The only place they feel at home is among other members of the third culture. As Ruth Hill Useem and Richard D. Downie have written, "Where they feel most like themselves is in that interstitial culture, the third culture, which is created, shared, and carried by persons who are relating societies, or sections thereof, to each other."[6] Other scholars have pointed out that expatriate families may have more in common with other expatriates than with nontraveled Americans, a situation that can cause them to become estranged from family ties and old friendships.[7]

Repatriates retain the characteristics of what social scientists refer to as the "stranger-group," the group of strangers in the same position. Strangers in a foreign environment feel insecure and have a strong need for affiliation with others. Neither home- nor host-country groups can meet their needs for affiliation and security, so they turn to other people in the same situation.[8] Anthropologist Dennison Nash alludes to this situation when he refers to the overseas American community (and, by extension, repatriated Americans) as "somewhere in limbo between home and host cultures."[9]

The feeling of being in a sort of limbo can be inferred from many of the comments of repatriates. "I do not feel comfortable with the Junior League set or the factory worker group," says one returnee. "I have felt very alone most of my adult life because the locals have a hard time liking people who have lived other places." Another repatriate echoes this thought: "I live in a rural area and I can't talk to the locals about crops or cows because I've had no experience with them just as the locals have no experience with living in a foreign country." Sometimes this feeling is coupled with a certain amount of disdain for the "monoculture" of the local community; more usually, however, it is simply a matter of not fitting in. "I fear that I will always be a stranger in my own country," says one returnee.

The feeling of not fitting in or having anything in common with the people in one's immediate environment causes some returnees to withdraw from an active social life. Ellen Turner, who returned to the States more than thirty-five years ago, explains: "I can't tell you whether I'm well integrated or not. I move through quite easily but I find a great need to work and be by myself away from the high-speed crowds. I have never felt I was totally at home anywhere I have lived as an adult. The best is back in the woods where I live in North Carolina."

Another returnee states this position more succinctly: "I've always been different, and the only society I'm going to really integrate with is the society that leaves me alone." These repatriates resemble the hero of Albert Camus's *The Stranger*, who, as Camus explained, "is condemned because he doesn't play the game. In this sense he is a stranger to the society in which he lives; he drifts in the margin."[10]

"Fitting in" evidently occurs, if at all, to varying degrees and in many different ways. But even the most fully integrated returnees sometimes feel like outsiders. Returnees often state that they feel integrated into "world" or "international" society rather than into American society. Having left behind the status of an American in a foreign country, Absentee Americans are reluctant to identify themselves as ordinary U.S. citizens. They often refer to themselves as global Americans, international Americans, or world citizens. In the words of one repatriate, "I feel as though I'm a member of a much larger community than one nation. Now it has come into vogue to talk about the 'global village' that I feel I've been a member of for most of my life." This notion of world citizenship is a distinctive characteristic of repatriates and is examined in detail in a later chapter.

Rebecca Sholes describes the process that many repatriates go through in coming to terms with their nationality: "I more readily identify myself as an American now than when I first came to the United States. However, I am quick to qualify this statement by telling people that I did not grow up here, particularly when asked where I am from. It is important to me to convey this to people as my 'nationality.' It helps to explain who I am. At the age of thirty-one, having lived in the United States for twelve years, I am still struggling with my 'American identity' and what that means to me. Initially I wanted to reject it, feeling that I was an American only because my parents were. Now, I accept it as a part of myself that has helped to shape who I am. As I get older, I find myself wanting to learn more about the United States and my family history in this country. This struggle for identity is a process I feel I will always be going through."

NOTES

1. Everett V. Stonequist, *The Marginal Man* (New York: Russell and Russell, 1937), pp. 3–4.

2. Stonequist, *The Marginal Man.*

3. E. D. Hirsch, Jr., Joseph F. Kett, and James Trefil, *The Dictionary of Cultural Literacy: What Every American Needs to Know* (Boston: Houghton Mifflin, 1988), p. ix.

4. Clyde N. Austin, "Descriptive Statements of Missionary Families," one-page handout, November 1, 1986.

5. E. D. Hirsch, Jr., *Cultural Literacy: What Every American Needs to Know* (Boston: Houghton Mifflin, 1987), p. 16.

6. Ruth Hill Useem and Richard D. Downie, "Third-Culture Kids," *Today's Education* (Sept.–Oct. 1976): 103.

7. Ted Ward, *Living Overseas: A Book of Preparations* (New York: Free Press, 1984).

8. Simon N. Herman and Erling O. Schild, "The Stranger-Group in a Cross-Cultural Situation," *Sociometry*, 24 (1961): 165–76.

9. Dennison Nash, *A Community in Limbo: An Anthropological Study of an American Community Abroad* (Bloomington: Indiana University Press, 1970).

10. Albert Camus, *The Stranger*, trans. Stuart Gilbert (New York: Knopf, 1946), preface.

5

THE RELATIVISTS

_____

Were it not for my time abroad, I would be a shadow of the person I now am.

It has affected every corner of my life and belief system: my love for ethnic foods, my impatience with suburban provincialism, my urge to travel, my sensitivity to different approaches to life, my ability to walk in another person's shoes, my contempt for the accumulation of personal wealth, my desire to be with people from other countries—to be broadened by their different perspectives.

Breathless Corners is a place near Karachi, Pakistan, where in the late 1950s thousands of squatters lived with their water buffalo in makeshift shacks created by hammering out beer and soda cans and joining them together to form walls. The residents survived by selling patties made from buffalo dung, which were used as fuel. Swarms of emaciated children surrounded passing cars and begged for coins.

Peter Nelson remembers Breathless Corners when people complain about minor inconveniences like riding an elevator that stops at every floor. "At least you don't have to sleep with your water buffalo," he thinks to himself.

To Absentee Americans, especially those who have lived in Third-World countries, the affluence of America is overwhelming. Many respondents said that when they returned to the United States they were struck by the material well-being of most Americans, along with their apparent tendency to want more, to shop constantly, and to throw away things that are no longer new. (One repatriate says that she hates to shop for clothes. People often give her clothes that are "very nice; they are just tired of them.") With surprising frequency returnees comment on how they feel about going into large supermarkets. "I am still, to this day, overwhelmed by supermarkets where they sell everything. I've seen too many people who are starving," says Nelson. Another returnee adds, "I am astounded by the huge parking lots surrounding the shopping malls which always seem full. Can this many people actually be in need of purchasing this many new things?"

These reactions to the sheer size and affluence of America are coupled with a feeling of discouragement at a level of consumption that is perceived as wasteful and self-indulgent. Returnees who have lived in Third-World countries are offended by Americans' casual acceptance of clean and plentiful water, electricity, food, and services of all kinds. Some have lived in places where people have to walk a mile to get water—yet they see Americans taking hot running water for granted—not to mention such amenities as electric can openers. Many also comment on the pollution resulting from excessive consumption.

CULTURAL RELATIVITY

Many repatriates say that living overseas has changed the way they look at the United States: "I learned that America is not always right in its actions in the international community"; "I think that living overseas opened my eyes to ways other than the 'American way.' I don't think that our way is necessarily the best way." This tendency to view the United States from the perspective of a foreigner is part of a constellation of traits that characterize many Absentee Americans. Chief among these is the awareness that "there is a world out there." This awareness goes beyond the old saying that "travel is broadening"; almost without exception, repatriates have a sense of cultural relativity, of the essential validity of all cultures, coupled with an immense respect for the cultures in which they have lived. One returnee says that life overseas made her aware of the "vast varieties of human kinds, enormous variety of human experiences."

Absentee Americans feel that they have a better understanding of people who are different, perhaps because they feel so different themselves, and that their capacity for empathy has been enhanced by living overseas. They are acutely aware of the sources of cultural differences—in educational systems, for example—and of the need for a basic respect for all human beings. Many also mention that being part of a white minority in countries like Kenya and Thailand opened their eyes to the situation of racial and ethnic minority groups in the United States, and that they feel able to interact more naturally with members of such groups as a result.

Returnees often comment that living abroad has enhanced their ability to understand the differences in issues and values between the first and third worlds, as well as between majority and minority (especially immigrant) groups in the United States. A returnee who spent her teenage years in Zaire says, "It made me aware of the enormous contrasts in opportunity and wealth between Africa and the United States and thus more aware of oppressed and unfortunate people in the United States." Another repatriate says, "Having grown up in the position of 'other,' I found I was very sensitive to the position of minorities in the United States." This is true even of repatriates who spent only one or two years overseas. The experience of living abroad during the teenage years appears to create a focal point in the person's memory and to serve as a basis of comparison for many later experiences. One returnee says, "Living in Brazil and seeing the horrible poverty there gave me a lifelong commitment to social and economic justice."

The flip side of returnees' sense of cultural relativity is an intensified awareness of ethnocentric tendencies among Americans. As one repatriate remarks, "We called Africans uncultured, when most school-age children spoke English, Swahili, and their tribal tongue, while most of the time we barely speak adequate English." A returnee whose childhood years were spent in a wide variety of settings, including Belgium, Vietnam, and Nigeria, sums up this feeling as follows: "The years abroad taught me to accept all peoples and I felt a part of a global community. I have always disliked America's ethnocentrism. Americans in the middle of another country still expect others to do it 'our' way."

At the same time, many repatriates have a heightened appreciation for the United States after living in more deprived societies; "I think it's a relative miracle when people are *not* oppressed, starving, and illiterate," says one. Returnees also develop a deep appreciation for the constitutional protection of individual rights and the relative lack of limits on personal freedom in this country. (Some tell of hair-raising episodes in which they experienced first-hand the infringements on individual rights that characterize some societies, such as Spain under the Franco regime.) They also comment on the relative stability of political life in the United States: "Having seen five coups in two years in Pakistan, it's nice to know the Democrats and Republicans are watching each other in this country." In some cases this greater appreciation is reflected in increased patriotism, but usually returnees' patriotic feelings are tempered by the belief that the United States is, or should be, a member of the world community.

Many returnees describe themselves as multicultural and pride themselves on being able to interact well with people from a variety of cultural backgrounds. They also are likely to know two or more languages and are willing to use language to break down cultural barriers; in most countries, an effort to use the host country's language will evoke a positive response. Indeed, returnees may unconsciously use words and phrases of languages learned overseas even when they are speaking to nonrepatriate friends and family members. In some cases Absentee Americans find themselves speaking nonidiomatic English upon their return to the United States, and it may take some time for them to adjust their phrasing and syntax.

The efforts made by Absentee Americans to learn other languages, if only to be able to make themselves understood by taxi drivers and shopkeepers, probably contribute to their strong sense of cultural relativity. One returnee says that "by listening to—and not understanding—different languages spoken I realized that we must sound funny to them too. I came to accept most of this as a cultural difference and I became more accepting once back here."

The Absentee American is involved with the idea of *cultures* as opposed to *culture*: The repatriate's world view tends to include elements of several national cultures in addition to that of the United States. In social-psychological parlance, the repatriate is heterocultural rather than monocultural.[1] Tennyson could have been referring to repatriates when he wrote, "I am a part of all that I have met." Returnees thus do not have a single cultural identity; they are cultural blends or "cultural chameleons." This trait is quickly recognized by other repatriates; when returnees meet, they tend to "click" immediately. This is one of the characteristics that have led social scientists to view repatriates as having a culture of their own, a "third culture."

Perhaps as an extension of their childhood experiences, repatriates tend to be interested in trying new foods, seeing new places, meeting people from other countries, and comparing the artistic expressions of different cultures. They also tend to be very attached to objects that represent other cultures. Sometimes called "sacred objects," these items are kept and displayed long after their owner has returned to the United States. A typical collection of sacred objects includes a straw hat from Lesotho, a peacock-feather fan from India, a Tibetan prayer wheel, painted ceramics from Rhodes, an abacus from Hong Kong, Thai shadow puppets, a carved impala from Tanzania, a wooden box shaped like a Swiss chalet, and a set of castanets. Sacred objects were not necessarily obtained in places where the repatriate has lived; they have come from many sources, often as gifts. They are not the souvenirs of the tourist; they are symbols of the repatriate's "native" environment.

AVOIDANCE OF ABSOLUTES

Along with greater tolerance and appreciation of cultural differences comes a certain impatience with nonreturnees who do not share this outlook. A prime target is failure to accept new or different ideas. As one repatriate remarks, "I became less tolerant of smug ignorance, confronting it when I consider it to be caused by a limited world view." Another says, "Believing what you believe in is great, as long as you realize another person may differ from you and as long as you don't force your view on someone else."

Returnees tend to be tolerant of ambiguity, nonjudgmental, and skeptical of absolutes. They have been brought up to question, to look at things from several angles and to respect differences. "Living overseas forced me to understand that there is more than one right answer," is a typical comment, along with "We were exposed to so many different cultures that there ended up being no one right way." According to one returnee, life overseas "showed me that there is a huge range of what is 'right, true, or obvious.' " Another adds, "My experience [overseas] taught me to search for multiple points of view."

For some, the result is a lack of commitment to any single religion or ethical philosopy. William Robb, who spent parts of his childhood in England and Pakistan, says, "I think I became more of a religious skeptic or agnostic after seeing two other major faiths close up." Another returnee says, "Living overseas, I came to realize all religion is one. I go to churches, temples, or even mosques, depending on my location." A third points out that "seeing so many other religions so absolutely positive that theirs

was the only true way, it became clear that there couldn't possibly
be one true religion, or for that matter, one absolute perspective
on anything."

Sometimes the lack of boundaries can result in an unconven-
tional imagination and an offbeat and idiosyncratic sense of
humor. Returnees are willing to take intellectual risks and tend
toward eclecticism and universalism in many areas, ranging from
music to politics. At the same time, the diversity of social customs to which Absentee Americans have been exposed makes it
difficult for them to take fads and trends very seriously. And their
appreciation of diversity makes them slow to pass judgment.

A major consequence of the tendency to try to see situations
from more than one angle is a reluctance to make categorical
statements; indeed, some repatriates admit to feeling confused in
an environment in which everyone else seems ready to express all
kinds of judgments. This is a major concern for Sherry Tousley, a
repatriate who now works as an intercultural consultant. "Having
seen the depth of conviction people all over the world have about
their beliefs," she comments, "I struggle with issues of 'knowing'
and 'truth.' I have both a longing to be at peace with 'knowing,'
and a great fear of it, a fear of dogma. I do have cultural assumptions and dogmas surrounding the subject of how to treat people,
how to *behave* as opposed to how to *believe*."

Tousley, whose father was a career army officer, was deeply
impressed by the devout beliefs and firm convictions held by
people in many other cultures. Although she had been raised in
a fundamentalist family and continues to believe in the existence
of a higher Being, she concluded that it is impossible to say that
any particular set of beliefs is right or true. At the same time, she
felt the need to create a belief system of her own. Her eventual
solution to this dilemma was to develop a "floating" belief system
that can incorporate values from different cultures or environments, continually reexamining them and discarding those that
no longer seem appropriate. Tousley spends a lot of time reading
about how other cultures view reality, looking for something that
will be meaningful for her. At any given time her belief system

is of necessity tentative in the same way that scientific theories are tentative. She admits that this can be uncomfortable at times, but she feels that it is a more sincere and realistic approach to life than dependence on a set of absolute "truths."

Tousley's views are echoed by Charlotte Hollis, who says that after returning to the United States from Pakistan she felt unable to return to her church. She says that she is "not atheistic or even confused. I just don't see it [religion] as real. There are too many other, conflicting views." Many returnees comment on the need to explore other belief systems besides those in which they were raised.

The same outlook extends to political beliefs. Although repatriates express admiration for the constitutional protections available to Americans and tend to favor democracy as a concept, they are also highly aware of flaws in the system. One returnee comments: "If our government worked as it is written, it would be the greatest government in the history of mankind. In many ways, it is the greatest government, but I am no longer blind to its faults, fallacies, and injustices." Expressing the duality that is characteristic of Absentee Americans, a number of repatriates describe themselves as "liberal conservatives."

The mind-opening effect of life overseas may be seen even in returnees who spent only two or three years abroad. One returnee says that her two and a half years in Thailand "opened my middle-class suburban mind with a crowbar." She become familiar with a variety of religions, philosophies, cultural attitudes, and viewpoints, and upon her return she changed her own religious affiliation: "My old church believed that if one did not accept Jesus Christ as the son of God, they would fry in Hell. This bothered my seventeen-year-old mind, in that I knew many highly spiritual people who were Muslim or Buddhist and I could not accept that God would send these gentle, kind people to Hell." She goes on to comment that her experience taught her to search for multiple points of view, to be accepting of differences, and to respect people from different cultures even when she disagrees with some of their attitudes.

These traits of repatriates can be understood as deriving from the experience of being a stranger both overseas and in the United States. As the social theorist Alfred Schutz explains, "Any member born or reared within the group accepts the ready-made standardized scheme of the cultural pattern handed down to him by ancestors, teachers, and authorities as an unquestioned and unquestionable guide in all the situations which normally occur within the social world." That pattern functions "to eliminate troublesome inquiries by offering ready-made directions for use, to replace truth hard to attain by comfortable truisms, and to substitute the self-explanatory for the questionable." This pattern is taken for granted by those raised within the group. But for others, such as immigrants or repatriates, this is not the case. "To [the stranger] the cultural pattern of the approached group does not have the authority of a tested system of recipes, and this, if for no other reason, because he does not partake in the vivid historical tradition by which it has been formed. . . . It has never become an integral part of his biography." As a result, "the cultural pattern of the appoached group is to the stranger not a shelter but a field of adventure, not a matter of course but a questionable topic of investigation."[2]

FOCUS ON THE INDIVIDUAL

Another key trait of Absentee Americans is a tendency to focus on the uniqueness of every individual—to accept people for who they are, not what they are. Nancy Blackmore, a graduate student at Harvard who grew up in Brazil, Uganda, and Kenya, emphasizes that for the repatriate cultural and ethnic differences are not significant in themselves. She points out that "cultural mainstreaming" occurs automatically in the overseas schools; during their formative years, children from numerous cultural and racial backgrounds are mixed together in nontraditional classrooms and given a great deal of individual attention. Diversity thus is a significant feature of the environment of American children overseas. In the words of an Absentee American whose childhood was spent in a variety of overseas settings, "Overseas, the foreign communities were small and everyone new was welcomed and accepted. It was okay to dress differently or have different norms because everyone had come from such diverse places. Socioeconomic background didn't seem to matter either. Ambassadors' children played with noncommissioned officers' children."

Blackmore notes that children who attend overseas schools tend not to perceive one another in terms of group membership, in contrast to the situation in American schools. Indeed, repatriates often express surprise at the cliquishness of American schoolchildren, considering it a typically American phenomenon. "The big question is, 'What are you?' " a black repatriate notes. "Overseas, I was an American. People either liked me or they didn't like me. . . . Here, the whole perspective is different. People look for classifications, and they tend to fear change or difference."[3]

It is difficult to put a finger on the source of this difference in attitudes. Perhaps it is as simple as the fact that all the children of Americans overseas attend the same schools, so that the effects of residential segregation are not felt. Most American communities overseas include people from a wide variety of backgrounds who work closely together, like it or not. The children thus are exposed to a model of social and ethnic integration. In many overseas communities the school attended by American children is an international school; students come into contact with many other ethnic and cultural groups, together with their beliefs and attitudes, not only within the school but in after-school social life.

Another possible explanation is the nomadic life-style of Absentee Americans. Having moved so often, the Absentee American has had to learn how to be included and accepted. Having been the new kid on the block over and over again, he or she has eventually translated the need to be accepted into a willingness to accept. Sharon Anderson, who attended DODDS schools in Japan and Germany as well as "on the mainland" (i.e., in the United States), reports that "we generally had few racial problems in our schools. We counted people as our friends due to factors such as personality, commonality of ideas, likes, dislikes, maturity, etc. Rank, color, culture did not influence who our chosen friends were." Moreover, "in a DOD overseas school you are the new kid for a day or two. In a civilian school [in the United States] you are the new kid all year long because these kids have formed their cliques in kindergarten!"

Tousley adds that people are naturally insecure and feel threatened by what is different. They therefore seek out those like themselves and avoid those who seem foreign or strange. The Absentee American, on the other hand, has such a strong need to be accepted that he or she will try to find a way to accommodate others. This trait is reflected in the comments of a repatriate who reports that "because there was such a constant turnover of people, I learned to look for the good in people as opposed to the faults and that way I could be friends quickly with anyone." Similarly, a returnee from Brazil says, "Hopefully I'm more open and accepting to differences in others, as for much of my youth I was the different one."

Returnees often mention the importance of respect for others. In addition, they emphasize the need to demonstrate that respect. Chuck Tigue, who spent three years in Spain, notes that the Spaniards are a very formal people and expect formality in interpersonal relations. If one respects this requirement, they respond positively. Like many repatriates, he espouses an intercultural version of what is sometimes called the Platinum Rule: Do unto others as they would have you do unto them. Understanding how to show courtesy in different cultural contexts, and then showing it, is crucial.

Parental influence is, of course, an important element in the repatriate's attitude toward diversity. The parents of Absentee Americans have been described as "highly educated or highly skilled people who are forging the networks that intertwine and interrelate the peoples of the world,"[4] and many make a strong effort to instill in their children an appreciation of diversity. "We were always encouraged to view the world as one community, and to see people for their unique qualities, rather than their

differences," says Jim Stedman, whose father was a regional
representative for the United Nations Development Programme.
"I do not recall ever having a sour racial or ethnic moment in my
life—and I owe much of that to my experience of living overseas,
and to our 'world house' upbringing." Another repatriate says,
"My reaction to life overseas was driven by the example my
parents set of complete acceptance of cross-cultural matters."

Most parents of Absentee Americans emphasize that they are
guests in the countries in which they are stationed. Indeed, a few
repatriates comment that they were expected to be "little ambassadors," a source, sometimes, of a feeling of always being on
display or living in a fishbowl. Social scientists who have studied
the life-style of American families overseas have drawn attention to this characteristic: "Behavior which is considered within
the area of 'privacy' and 'nobody's business' within the United
States becomes redefined in the foreign setting as visible 'public'
behavior and 'everybody's business' . . . . [Absentee Americans]
are not just individuals relating themselves privately to each other
within the confines of their own home, but living examples of
America."[5] The efforts of parents to ensure that their children will
behave appropriately in the host country leads them to emphasize
respect for the individual and the importance of making an effort
to get along with people from a variety of backgrounds.

IMPORTANCE OF FAMILY AND FRIENDS

Friendships take on great significance for the returnee, especially friendships with other repatriates. In all their friendships
returnees stress commitment, perhaps because friendships serve
as a partial substitute for the roots they lack. As David Pollock
explains, "the third-culture kid finds rootedness in relationships,
not geography." But the importance of friendships also derives
from the experience of living overseas. For example, numerous
scholars have remarked on the tendency of American families
overseas to become more cohesive. Not only do family members spend more time together because of their relative isolation

from other American families, but family cohesiveness may serve as a defense against the anxiety experienced when one lives in a strange culture. According to sociologists Ruth Useem and Richard Downie, family members overseas "share the common experience of moving into unfamiliar territory and offer each other mutual support in the face of change and strangeness. Parents are often the only people with whom [third-culture kids] have a continuing relationship as they move from one location to another."[6] In addition, the representational role of American families overseas leads to increased emphasis on family interaction.[7]

Besides family influences, there are the effects of being part of a relatively isolated community. The child in a military or Foreign Service post is usually part of a small and continually changing group. In many overseas communities and schools there is little choice about group membership, and it is almost impossible to form cliques. Lacking other companions, the children form close ties to one another, ties that may last long after all of them have been transferred to other posts or back to the United States. The increase in the frequency and intensity of reunions among overseas-school alumni in recent years is a logical outcome of this tendency.

A paradoxical aspect of returnees is that, despite their adaptability and ease in forming friendships overseas, they may be slow to form lasting friendships or emotional attachments after returning to the United States. They have too often experienced the "gut wrenching" that occurs when they, or their close friends, have left one post for another, and they may be unwilling to make the effort to make new friends. "I would get so sad when I had to leave my friends," one teenage returnee says. "And each time you do it, it gets harder and harder. . . . Saying good-bye is so hard because you know you'll probably never see these people again. . . . You get to the place you don't want to make friends anymore."[8]

Psychologists have devoted some attention to the difficulties experienced by repatriates in achieving intimacy. Although this subject is beyond the scope of this book, it appears that frequent moves during the teenage years can have a detrimental effect on the ability to maintain intimate relationships; the young person has not developed the skills to maintain such relationships. Another important factor is differences in school size: "Relationships that develop in our large educational institutions in the U.S., where 'connectedness' may not exist once school is out for the day, may be quite different than [those that develop] overseas, where school, community and social life are often intertwined."[9] Many repatriates comment that their spouse and closest friends are people who also lived overseas, to whom they feel that they can reveal their true selves. They also say that they lack a "best" friend.

A GLOBAL ORIENTATION

Living outside the United States seems to have given returnees an unusually broad world view and a heightened interest in and sensitivity to world affairs. As one repatriate explains, "I think in global terms. The simple fact of physically living in other countries opens up your thought process to include the larger earth and all its problems." Another says, "I feel that I have a broader base of experience to draw on than the average American when it comes to social and political issues."

One source of this expanded world view is the experience of having actually witnessed the impact of U.S. policies on other nations. Says Ronald Gordon, a former international planning manager who grew up in the Foreign Service, "I have a better perspective on the views and actions of other countries. I do not necessarily agree, but I have empathy for positions at variance with the United States." "I tend to want to know what Japanese, French, German, and Chinese opinions are on whatever issue is in the forefront of the news," adds another repatriate.

To some extent, returnees' global orientation stems from the ability to visualize other countries as real places. As one repatriate expresses it, "I have mental pictures of people behind the statistics they give on the news about Africa and Europe.

My experience there allows me to speak out about effective and culturally appropriate economic aid to Third-World countries."

In part, the Absentee American has a global view because it is difficult or impossible for him or her to have a local view. "Being rootless, we didn't have social responsibility for the community," says one repatriate. He says he cannot take local politics seriously because he has been conditioned to concentrate on larger issues of national and world politics.

Many returnees express surprise at Americans' apparent lack of interest in geography, languages, or foreign affairs. They continually encounter contemporaries who believe India is a variant of Indiana, or that Chinese is spoken in Tokyo, or that people who live in Africa have lions running around in their backyards. Repatriates react with curiosity, rather than fear or lack of interest, to the foreign. Many come from families in which every new overseas assignment was an adventure and an opportunity. They retain this sense of adventure in adulthood through continued interest in other countries (as well as other areas of the United States) and concern about the United States' relations with the rest of the world. Repatriates' careers reflect these interests; many returnees find employment in such fields as anthropology or U.S. diplomatic history.

Finally, many repatriates are concerned about the American tendency to feel that the United States is the best or greatest nation in the world, whether one is referring to products, philosophies, social theories, or whatever, They note, however, that nationalism is not unique to the United States. Most believe that globalism is preferable to nationalism and that efforts to create a healthy global economy and environment are hampered by misguided national interests, ethnocentrism, and territoriality.

NOTES

1. Stephen Bochner, ed. *The Mediating Person: Bridges Between Cultures* (Boston: G. K. Hall, 1981).

2. Alfred Schutz, "The Stranger: An Essay in Social Psychology," in *Collected Papers*, ed. Arvid Brodersen (The Hague: Martinus Nijhoff, 1964), Vol. 2, pp. 95, 96, 104.

3. Quoted in Claire Kittredge, "Growing Up Global," *Boston Globe Magazine*, April 3, 1988.

4. Ruth Hill Useem and Richard Downie, "Third-Culture Kids," *Today's Education* (Sept.–Oct. 1976): 103.

5. Ruth Useem, "The American Family in India," *Annals of the American Academy of Political and Social Sciences, 368* (1966): 134.

6. Useem and Downie, "Third-Culture Kids." See also Dennison Nash, *A Community in Limbo: An Anthropological Study of an American Community Abroad* (Bloomington: Indiana University Press, 1970).

7. Useem, "The American Family in India."

8. Quoted in Eakin, *The Foreign Service Teenager—At Home in the U.S.: A Few Thoughts for Parents Returning with Teenagers* (Washington, D.C.: Overseas Briefing Center, Foreign Service Institute, U.S. Department of State, May 1988), p. 45.

9. Ibid., p. 20.

6

THE GLOBAL CITIZENS

I am not a Virginian, but an American.

—Patrick Henry

When people ask me where I am from (what state), I tell them I don't have a home state but my father and mother were from South Dakota and that is where I went to college. However, if that was asked of me overseas by a native I would tell them America; I have lived all over it. As far as what it signifies to me, I don't care about nationality. But I am proud of my heritage.

Although most repatriates acknowledge their United States citizenship, they are ambivalent about the idea of being "an American," even twenty or more years after returning to the States. It's as if the formation of a national identity cannot be completed—or perhaps the Absentee American has, however unconsciously, formed an international identity during childhood. One repatriate sums up this feeling as follows: "Basically, I consider myself international. I feel partial to many cultures and therefore am many nationalities in one."

For many repatriates the stigma of "the ugly American" is a very real problem. They comment often on the less than sterling qualities of American tourists whom they have encountered overseas (although they are quick to add that these traits are by no means universal). They note that when they travel abroad they are often embarrassed to be identified as American and prefer to blend in with the host culture or at least keep others guessing about their nationality. Some comment that they hope to show people of other nations that there are sensitive, respectful Americans as well as "the other kind."

The Absentee American's ambivalence about nationality is expressed in various ways. Some repatriates say that they are Americans only by happenstance or because there is no other convenient and/or meaningful label that is easily understood by others. Others draw a distinction between being a U.S. citizen and being an American. Still others think of themselves as citizens of other nations as well as the United States, even though they may not actually hold dual citizenship. When asked "Do you readily identify yourself as an American?" respondents often answered "yes and no" or "I guess so." Donald James, a public-affairs specialist at NASA who spent much of his childhood in Ghana, Thailand, and Kenya, comments: "I feel I am an American, but not to the exclusion of other countries, cultures, or people." Another returnee says that he is "many nationalities in one."

Absentee Americans who spent a large portion of their childhood in a single country often developed a strong identification with that country. Diane Terry, who spent most of her early years in Kenya, is typical. "I think of myself as being Kenyan," she says. Kenya "is where the majority of my memories are." She considers herself very lucky to be an American, but says, "I still consider myself to be Kenyan, because that's where my heart is."

In some cases uneasiness about being an American has a moral or philosophical basis. As one repatriate remarks, "The *ideals* of this country continue to amaze me; the actual practice and realization of these goals is difficult and often dubious." Another returnee says, "I owe my allegiance to the Constitution of the United States and not to any government. Our system may not be perfect, but it's better than any other that I have experienced."

Repatriates who say that they consider themselves Americans tend to add various qualifications and exceptions, as if to make it clear that they are not "true" or typical Americans or that they are "slightly un-American." Often they say that they are Americans because they cannot come up with another label that would be appropriate. They may view themselves as mixtures, like Stacey Grosvenor, who describes herself as "a combination of American traits on the outside and European views on the inside." Pat Wilson, who attended high school in Thailand and now advises students who wish to study abroad, says, "Of course I am an American. However, I am also a 'mixture' of two different cultures, and sometimes finding my identity in between those two cultures has been difficult." Other repatriates say that although they identify themselves as Americans, they feel comfortable only when they are between cultures or with others who share their experience. "Yes, I am an American," says one returnee, "but this American would rather live outside the United States."

Returnees from bicultural or nonwhite families are especially likely to place themselves in a hyphenated category—African-American, European-American, Mexican-American, and so on. Tina Melendez says, "I view myself as an American *citizen* that is half American, half Puerto Rican. Yes, I'm an American but with two cultures that define *me*." On the other hand, returnees who were born overseas often have an acute sense of divided citizenship or dual nationality: "I am an American (as well as a Brazilian)"; "I am a Brazilian at heart, but love the United States." Similar feelings are expressed by those who spent their entire childhood overseas. One returnee who was subject to the draft three weeks after coming to the United States from Africa says that he was extremely reluctant to serve a country that he barely knew.

Those who find it difficult to identify themselves as Americans sometimes compare themselves to the "man without a country." Many refer to themselves as global nomads or third-culture kids first and Americans second. Those who spent many years in England or Europe may describe themselves as "continental." Some note that they often find themselves talking about Americans in the third person, and they may "commute" between the United States and a chosen country such as Germany.

THE IDEA OF WORLD CITIZENSHIP

Many Absentee Americans emphasize the importance of being a citizen of the earth—or of the universe—first and of a nation second, if at all: "I consider myself a human being who happens to live in America" is a typical comment. Repatriates frequently refer to themselves as global or international citizens (or as world citizens who happen to live in the United States, or as having joint citizenship in the United States and the world) and comment that they could probably live quite happily almost anywhere in the world. One returnee says that she is a "child of the world" and as such could be comfortable in almost any culture. Another says, "If passports for global citizens or citizens of the world were issued, I would probably go for one." A third says that he prefers to think of himself as "a Terran; a citizen of the globe." Even those who are unequivocal about being Americans may refer to themselves as "worldly Americans" and say that they would like to live in and expand their knowledge of other countries. Many say that they feel a responsibility to the world at large and to the planet: "Our planet as a whole needs to be cared for and that is where our loyalties should lie."

Sometimes nationality is viewed as a convenience; returnees may identify themselves as Americans in some situations and not in others: "Depends on which country I'm in and who I'm talking to." "I readily identify myself as an American wherever it is prudent to do so," comments Tony Karian. "I also readily identify myself as an African or European whenever appropriate. I was wandering alone in Egypt several years ago and let myself be held up at machine-gun point by a lone soldier. My jabbering in Swahili convinced him that I was indeed another poor African."

Tony's brother Michael comments that he still doesn't feel very American and, indeed, would change his citizenship if he could find a nation whose policies are more compatible with his views. Nationality per se is not important to him.

A step beyond this feeling is the belief that nationality is absurd. This opinion is rarely voiced but seems to underlie the ambivalence expressed by many returnees. "I am a citizen of spaceship Earth, if you like," says Richard Schaefer, an artist-composer who grew up in India, Thailand, and Kenya. Political activist Ella Seneres, who spent her childhood in Mexico, Japan, England, and Kenya, says "I consider myself a Planetary Rainbow Warrior. I pledge myself to the earth, to the web of life."

Absentee Americans' feeling of world citizenship is reflected in the kinds of experiences they wish to provide for their children. "I do my best to instruct my own family with the world community vision that I was raised with," says one. Other returnees comment that they hope to give their children the experience of living overseas so that they can "see America from the outside."

PRIDE IN AMERICA

Some returnees have no trouble identifying themselves as Americans. For them, the pride of being an American—and the sense of privilege—outweighs any qualms they may have about the actions of the United States relative to other nations. "I'm proud of it," says a returnee who spent her teenage years in Kenya. "It signifies for me a place that you can at least try to fight for what you believe." Another, who returned from Belgium a few years ago, says, "Living elsewhere has made me feel more strongly that I'm American and proud of it." This pride is often accompanied by gratitude for the personal freedoms—especially freedom of speech—associated with American citizenship, and a feeling of irritation with those who take these freedoms for granted. Many returnees comment that freedom includes the freedom to disagree (a freedom that they exercise rather frequently). One returnee sums up this point of view as follows: "The major significance of being an American is the freedom—within bounds—to live my life as I choose; to have opportunities for growth and success; and not live in a country where armed conflict is a way of life."

Even for those who express such feelings, pride is sometimes mixed with embarrassment. "I try not to make excuses to foreign visitors for our government," remarks John Littlefield, whose father's Air Force career took him to Japan, Germany, and England, "but I am sometimes embarrassed to admit my heritage when we have pulled some incredibly dumb stunt." Laura Minor expresses a similar view. She is not proud of the way the United States acts toward the rest of the world, but she cannot imagine being a citizen of any other nation.

Absentee Americans who express pride in the United States as a democracy often say that their pride is accompanied by a sense of responsibility. They say that it is important to vote, pay taxes, and be informed about and participate in the affairs of the nation in order to preserve the privileges it offers. One repatriate comments: "I have become more aware of our rights and responsibilities accorded us by our form of government, because I have been among people who did not have these rights and privileges." Another says that for her the significance of being an American has changed over time: "It used to make me feel superior . . . now it is a responsibility."

Returnees often note that they are awed by the standard of living that is viewed as completely normal in the United States. Many say that they feel lucky. "I used to speculate on the karma that placed some of us in the United States at birth," says one. "Being an American was always the best card to have been dealt."

THE PROBLEM OF PATRIOTISM

Patriotism is a controversial issue for returnees; many comment that they do not consider themselves patriots. "Patriotism to me is exclusive—'my country *above* yours,' win/lose," says Donald James. Others express concern about "flag-waving": "I'm always amazed to see the U.S. flag flying from front porches and wonder why people feel the need to declare their nationalism." Howard Beardslee says that patriotism has a tendency to block out common sense; he describes himself as "measuredly patriotic." Other repatriates express qualms about seeing the flag used as a symbol of supremacy: "I'm an American by birth. But I don't see myself as a citizen of the 'best' country in the world. When I see too much flag waving it worries me. There have been times while living overseas that I've had to keep a low profile as an American."

Many returnees are concerned about the "my country right or wrong" philosophy. They appreciate the nation's ideals and its good qualities, but they are far from believing that it is infallible. Their outlook is summed up in a paraphrase by former Representative Carl Schurz: "My country right or wrong: when right, to be kept right, when wrong, to be put right." They are, in short, not ashamed to be Americans, but ashamed of departures from the nation's ideals.

On the other hand, some returnees express strong patriotic feelings: "I enjoy military parades, patriotic shows, cry when a good chorus sings 'America the Beautiful.' " "I cry when the American flag goes by in a parade and when I see the armed forces march." Many note how moved they were upon seeing the Statue of Liberty when they returned to the United States. A repatriate who spent her childhood in Iraq and Brazil remarks, "I remember the primitive circumstances to which we adapted.

I realized how blessed I am and I get disgusted with grumbling nonpatriots. I want to *ex*patriate them—to send them off to Uganda or China to taste what oppression *really* is."

Even returnees who do not readily identify themselves as Americans sometimes admit to a "knee-jerk patriotism," especially on memorable occasions like the Olympics, space shuttle launches, and the release of the American hostages from Iran in 1981. This sudden chauvinistic reaction is especially intense when the United States is seriously threatened or humiliated. One returnee describes this feeling as follows: "Even if a violent reaction to American policies seems justified, even if America deserves to get kicked in the pants sometimes, I hurt inside when it happens." He also says that he shared the national joy over the American victories in the 1984 Olympics, not because of the medals won but because of the United States' performance as a nation. It appears that the experience of representing the United States overseas has created an unconscious yearning for a national identity; when the nation itself appears to be unified, the repatriate feels this need most intensely. One returnee expresses this feeling quite simply: "I have always considered myself an American wherever I have been and I am unwilling to lose that one sense of belonging I have."

Most Absentee Americans believe that all the people on earth are one family—the human tribe. But they recognize that from a practical standpoint nationality, or at least citizenship, is unavoidable. "We've all got to live in a certain corner of the world," says William Robb. "This creates differences—in language, in priorities, in feelings about how best to live one's life. I identify myself as an American, and I love my country. Sometimes this is unfortunate because it puts me in opposition to citizens of other nations."

Like many returnees, Robb recognizes that nationality is a basic form of self-definition and that it has emotional overtones. Even repatriates usually cannot imagine being a citizen of another nation. The trick is to find ways to make nationality less divisive. Robb is hopeful that the European Community will show the world how national divisions can be overcome. "If that incredible collection of cultures and languages can defy historical precedent and build a new nation," he says, "so can the rest of us."

7

THE WANDERERS

Breathes there the man, with soul so dead,
Who never to himself hath said
"This is my own, my native land!"
Whose heart hath ne'er within him burned,
As home his footsteps he hath turned
From wandering on a foreign strand?

—Walter Scott

In Edward Everett Hale's classic story, *The Man Without a Country*, Philip Nolan, who has been sentenced to permanent exile aboard ships of the U.S. Navy, inadvertently reads Scott's lines and is overcome by grief and remorse. His sentence stemmed from an outburst during his trial on charges of treason: "Damn the United States! I wish I may never hear of the United States again!" Few Absentee Americans experience such extremes of emotion regarding their native land. But many, perhaps most, experience a sort of steady, low-level tension between the desire to wander and the yearning for "home."

The lack of a fully formed national identity can have a significant effect on the personality. Everett Stonequist pointed to this possibility in *The Marginal Man*:

> [The] evolution of personality takes place most easily and spontaneously when the individual . . . lives in a reasonably stable and organized society. Tradition and custom then chart the course of his career. . . . He has but one tribal or national tradition to acquire, one language to learn, one political loyalty to develop. . . . The unity and harmony of the social system are reflected in the unity and harmony of his personality. . . . Thus his personal sentiments will mirror the sentiments of his society. . . . His conception of himself will have a core of certainty paralleling the certainty of his group membership.[1]

The repatriate's background is the exact opposite of this formulation. Nomadic rather than stable, diverse rather than unified, the Absentee American's life-style may be reflected in rootlessness and restlessness during the returnee's adult years. Like the marginal man, the Absentee American is "poised in psychological uncertainty between two (or more) social worlds; reflecting in his soul the discords and harmonies, repulsions and attractions of those worlds."[2]

The experience of growing up overseas seems to have given many returnees a need to keep moving—an "itchy foot" or wanderlust. As Peter Nelson says, "Home is where I unpack my Pan Am bag—where I'm living at that moment. 'Roots' is a foreign concept to me." Nelson says he could "leave tomorrow with no regrets." Where would he go? "I'd go overseas in a heartbeat."

Many repatriates feel restless and unsettled. They believe they are unable to establish permanent roots, yet at the same time they express a desire to do so. They experience a conflict between the desire to understand the community in which they are living and a yearning for new experiences in other cultures. Some admit to wanting to establish roots but not knowing how—not knowing how to be a good neighbor, for example, or how to relate to friends over the long haul. Others, perhaps suffering from an overdose of change during childhood, find it hard to move as adults, yet long for contact with other cultures at home and abroad. "Every time (which is quite often) I am reminded of having lived abroad," says Marian Adams, "I want to return." Adams, a daughter of missionaries, herself went to India as a missionary in her young-adult years.

Some repatriates satisfy their need for frequent change by constantly traveling, rearranging their furniture, or changing hairstyles. Many others change jobs with great frequency, or gravitate toward freelance careers in which they can fulfill their need for variety. For them, as one returnee expresses it, "change has become a constant."

A significant number of Absentee Americans go overseas again as adults. They may join the Foreign Service or the military or the Peace Corps, or be assigned to a foreign city as a representative of a private firm or organization. A few choose to become expatriates. Many more returnees are attracted to careers with an international component—as translators or intercultural consultants, for example—or simply travel overseas whenever they get the chance. As one repatriate explains, "My childhood experiences have given rise to a craving to travel and visit places I've not yet seen."

Diane Anderson felt this craving so strongly that she found a job in customer service for TWA that provides extensive travel benefits. In the course of several short trips to Guatemala and other Latin American countries, she became deeply interested in problems and situations in those countries. She interviewed government officials and local leaders (she is also a freelance journalist), visited remote villages, and learned as much as she could about the politics and economics of the region. One thing led to another, and before long she found herself pulling strings to obtain a bulldozer for a Guatemalan communal farm so the farmers could build a road that would enable them to transport their coffee to market.

REENTRY AND STRANGER ANXIETY

For some returnees, the decision to work or live overseas is a reaction to the trauma of reentry. One returnee says that when he returned to the United States, "My former girlfriend told me I was a namedropper and she never wanted to see me again. My culture shock and homesickness for Thailand was intense enough for a psychiatrist to suggest that I return to Thailand. My business now takes me between Thailand and the United States several times a year and I always feel more comfortable in Thailand."

Repatriates who report such experiences appear to have suffered an especially acute case of what social scientists call stranger anxiety. As Dennison Nash describes it, "People who become strangers find themselves in a situation in which their subjective world is threatened by a lack of external confirmation. To the extent that they require such confirmation they will become uncertain and anxious about themselves and their behavior."[3] The stranger in a foreign setting becomes disoriented; familiar and meaningful points of reference are lacking, and a feeling of anomie results: "The points of reference which have become part of his inner world no longer receive the constant confirmation from experience which he had come to take for granted at home."[4] Tourists who have gotten lost in a city they have never visited before may have this experience; Absentee Americans, however, are "strangers in their own land." The shock of this discovery can be so intense that the repatriate is forever changed.

The following description of the impact of being a stranger was written with "foreign" countries in mind. But it is equally applicable (if not more so) to the impact of reentry:

The essence of the stranger's experience is *anomie*. Regardless of the foreign country to which a person migrates, we surmise that he is likely to experience, first, the condition of normlessness, or meaninglessness (acute *anomie*) and later, the condition of value contradiction or conflict (simple *anomie*). Depending on his sensitivity and his ability to tolerate such conditions, he will tend to experience stranger anxiety. This anxiety will then become a more or less significant motivating factor in his overseas life. It will persist until he finds or works out an acceptable role which eliminates *anomie* and enables him to feel at home in the foreign situation.[5]

Some returnees become quite discouraged about the prospect of ever feeling at home in American society. Marian Adams comments that she did not feel part of American society "until I'd been through ten years of counseling, a divorce, and many difficulties adjusting to jobs outside of the church." Another returnee, Circe Woessner, says, "Even after having lived there [in the United States] for six years, I tend to cling to my European ways. I do not feel comfortable there; however, I am not totally comfortable in Europe any more, either. I feel as though I am embracing two countries, two life-styles, and I don't fit in either place."

Woessner, a freelance artist and book illustrator, had a particularly difficult time when she returned to the United States for college: "Within the first six months I lived there [at age nineteen], I had only a job in a go-go bar to look forward to. I couldn't get any other work. I was held at gunpoint, 'kidnapped' by a crazy classmate, saw a person get shot, experienced racial prejudice, etc. . . . I had envisioned a life with a job, car, friends and college—all out of *American Graffiti*. Instead, no one liked me—they thought I was stuck-up. We had nothing in common. I found that the U.S. was a cold, superficial kind of place."

Woessner returned to West Germany, where she had spent most of her childhood. Despite the experiences just described, she says that she becomes angry when she encounters anti-American sentiment. She feels that she can see "both sides of the story" and enjoys being able to "straddle both cultures."

Another returnee relates a similar experience—although she eventually settled in the United States: "I never had any roots in this country. I continued to be drawn to the foreign; sought out foreign students in school; was better able to communicate with them; later married a foreigner. Finally I discovered the Foreign Service, which got me back out into the world. After eleven years out I have opted for early retirement (probably because my last post—Frankfurt—was too much like living in America). As for my finally settling down in this small town in Florida, who knows how long it will last?"

Britton Gildersleeve, who spent her childhood years in Vietnam and Thailand, describes some of the factors that led her to seek opportunities to live outside the United States. "My reentry was incredibly rocky. For my first summer at university I associated only with foreign students, and felt ashamed to admit I was American. I would only date foreign students, and spoke only French other than in class. . . . I remember very poignantly when I discovered the word 'expatriate.' It was as if I had come home. . . . My husband and I have chosen to become expatriates ourselves, and are raising a second generation of wanderers. . . . I am raising my children to feel 'American' in so far as they are able, but I do stress the benefits of their international experience."

Repatriates like Woessner and Gildersleeve illustrate the link between the stranger and the wanderer. As the sociologist Georg Simmel pointed out,

> The stranger is . . . the *potential* wanderer: Although he has not moved on, he has not quite overcome the freedom of coming and going. He is fixed within a particular spatial group. . . . But his position in this group is determined, essentially, by the fact that he has not belonged to it from the beginning, that he imports qualities into it, which do not and cannot stem from the group itself.[6]

In extreme cases the stranger/wanderer becomes an expatriate.

OVERSEAS CAREERS

Not all repatriates who live abroad were alienated by the reentry experience. For many, living and working overseas has always been a major life goal. A study of 150 repatriates enrolled in college who had spent at least one year abroad during their teens found that none wished to pursue a career exclusively in the United States. One-fourth named a place overseas where they would like to work; 29 percent expressed interest in following an overseas-based occupation; 25 percent wanted to be headquartered in the United States with periodic assignments abroad; and 12 percent wanted to be employed in the United States but have opportunities for job-related overseas travel. Only 7 percent reported feeling "at home" in the United States; 74 percent said they felt most comfortable with people who are internationally oriented and have lived abroad.[7]

Living abroad in adulthood appears to solidify the attitudes developed during childhood years spent overseas. Many repatriates say that living overseas as an adult reinforced the feeling that it is a privilege to be an American. One returnee comments: "Going back to Brazil to work after college brought home to me exactly how much I am an American and how I depend upon the social and political freedoms and economy of this country. I am far from the repulsive extreme of 'America, love it or leave it'; I think the privilege of being an American means working to improve life in this country and caring for people around the world." Another says, "I have often felt guilty for my privileged life as I walked among impoverished, desperate refugees in Hong Kong, on the Czech border in Germany, in Taiwan—all who would have given anything to call themselves American." Returnees often note that they have lived in countries where human rights are ignored, dissent is not tolerated, and democracy is an unattainable dream.

Other returnees echo these thoughts: "To me, the American system is still the world's best—for personal freedoms, for economic opportunities, for self-advancement, for richness in lands and natural resources, and for that still-existing reservoir of good will toward others. There are many flaws as well, but there's an admirable willingness to face them and experiment with solutions."

Returnees who spend additional time overseas as adults have opportunities to compare their childhood impressions with actual conditions, both abroad and in the United States. They tend to become more analytical and less emotional in their evaluation of the United States relative to other nations. Thus, a returnee who spent his working years setting up international operations for United Parcel Service notes that many people in other countries express a desire to emigrate, often to the United States, whereas relatively few Americans wish to live elsewhere. He and other adult "wanderers" express appreciation for the civil liberties and high level of living available in the United States, a strong respect for democracy, a realistic understanding of other countries' cultures and policies, and recognition of the limits on U.S. influence overseas.

There is a note of sadness in the comments of many of these returnees. They recognize the United States' good qualities but feel that those qualities are not adequately conveyed to the people of other nations. Judith Kifer's remarks are typical: "The United States is like a naive adolescent—good at heart, but often too wrapped up in its own problems and ignorant that other nations can perceive ideas in very different ways. The United States values material success and models this to itself and the world. Americans have other values—such as strength of character, morality, courage, and generosity—but they often fail to promote these qualities." Kifer, who entered the Christian ministry and lived in Germany and Switzerland for several years, believes that it is important for Americans who have lived in other countries to attempt to bridge this cultural gap.

Repatriates are unequivocal in their belief that there is no substitute for the experience of living overseas as a means of developing an understanding and appreciation of the attitudes, feelings, and expectations of people outside the United States. Many say that they wish or intend to raise their children overseas. Some cannot imagine bringing up a child in only one culture; they view such an upbringing as a handicap. A few, however, note that they would not stay overseas indefinitely; they wish their children to appreciate the unique qualities of American culture as well as those of other countries. Others express the belief that it is important for children to grow up in a stable environment with family and friends, particularly in the teenage years.

It is this outlook that has led some scholars to question the notion of a "third culture." As Nash points out,

> To say simply that Americans abroad . . . inhabit a "Third Culture" may tend to obscure the often complex transactions which lead to the positioning of an overseas community somewhere in limbo between home and host cultures. It also may convey the mistaken impression that most American overseasmen acquire a political allegiance to a "Third Culture" when, in fact, they have not given up their conscious or unconscious commitment to the United States and its overseas interests.[8]

In sum, however much Absentee Americans wander during adulthood, and even when they spend long periods of their lives overseas, they appear to retain a small compartment in their psyche that resembles the cabin of Philip Nolan in *The Man Without a Country*, in which "the stars and stripes were triced up above and around a picture of Washington, and he had painted a majestic eagle . . . [He] saw my glance and said . . . 'Here, you see, I have a country!' "

NOTES

1. Everett V. Stonequist, *The Marginal Man* (New York: Russell and Russell, 1937), pp. 1–2.

2. Ibid., p. 8.

3. Dennison Nash, *A Community in Limbo* (Bloomington: Indiana University Press, 1970), p. 109.

4. Ibid., p. 169.

5. Ibid., p. 188.

6. Georg Simmel, "The Stranger," in *The Sociology of Georg Simmel*, trans. and ed. Kurt H. Wolff (New York: Free Press, 1950), p. 402.

7. Reported in Ruth Hill Useem and Richard D. Downie, "Third-Culture Kids," *Today's Education* (Sept.-Oct. 1976).

8. Nash, *A Community in Limbo*, p. 201.

8

A MATTER OF
PERSPECTIVE

---

*Americans have a tendency to want to "Americanize" the world;
i.e., our beliefs and attitudes are always the best. In general, we
don't seem to be able to accept the uniqueness of other countries
and their people—we want to "fix" everything!*

*It is a pity that most Americans do not really have a firsthand
chance to live abroad with an open mind. It makes this country
look better, but it teaches us to be more critical of the United
States as well.*

Absentee Americans have been raised to be outsiders and obser-
vers. They look on the United States in the same way that they
look on other nations, from the perspective of an outsider looking
in. Much of the time they don't like what they see. They are
perturbed by what they perceive as the United States' "overbear-
ing," "arrogant," "self-righteous," "bullying," and/or "imperialistic" behavior toward other nations. The following statement is
typical: "I feel that the United States often takes on the role of

Big Brother too much and seems to feel entitled to interfere with the internal affairs of foreign countries with a general disregard for or lack of understanding of that country's culture and history. It is my impression that the United States feels that because it is a world power, its way is the best way regardless of whether it fits in with another country's cultural differences."

Some respondents feel that the very fact that the United States becomes involved in the affairs of other nations is by definition ethnocentric, if not imperialistic. They point out that the results rarely justify the investment; this applies both to monetary aid and to military intervention. The Big Brother or Global Policeman image comes up often. Many repatriates feel that the United States lacks adequate respect for the sovereignty of other nations—that it has the attitude of a colonial power—and that the resentment generated by its actions often leads to the scapegoating of Americans overseas.

Martha Opdahl, whose family lived in numerous countries in Asia and South America while she was growing up, says that she is outraged at the United States' "bullying posture toward all other nations—everything must go its way, or else." She feels "outrage and disbelief" when she hears about the U.S. government considering overt (let alone covert) interference and intervention in other nations' affairs. "Leave them alone! The U.S. is not the barometer of how life should be lived."

Many returnees are especially concerned by the United States' record of opposing communism without regard to the precise nature of a given "communist" regime's policies or public support (although they may feel that opposition to communism in general is justified). As Howard Beardslee points out, this criterion "allows us to support dictators the likes of Somoza, the Shah of Iran, Marcos, and Panama's Noriega. The dramatic turmoil following the eventual overthrow of these dictators sets the stage for anti-Americanism. We seem unable to learn from repetitions of this error." Another repatriate points out that the U.S. role is ambiguous—"one of defending democracies and also maintaining the status quo (i.e., elites)." This view is summed up in the following comment: "I get the feeling that Washington is like a large rock sitting on uneven ground in a stream so when you put your foot on it there is this unsteady rocking feeling and you're not sure which end is going to protrude out of the water."

Some repatriates point out that the United States does not appear as noble in the view of other nations as it does in its own. From the perspective of those nations, the United States is guided almost entirely by expediency. It does not maintain relations with nations in which it does not have an economic or strategic interest, and it provides minimal aid to Third-World nations. Repatriates also express concern about the inconsistencies in U.S. policy toward other nations. As Chuck Tigue points out, "The people of the United States denounce apartheid in South Africa, but ignore the mass killings in Argentina, Colombia, and Central America." And while the United States is generally quick to condemn aggressive acts by other nations, "the United States did not get excited when Libya invaded Chad (probably because most Americans could not find Chad on a map)." Many repatriates point to the need for a consistent policy with regard to aggressive nations, or simply for a policy of nonintervention.

NEED FOR INTERCULTURAL CONTACT

Absentee Americans are especially troubled by the failure of most Americans to make an effort to understand the culture and point of view of people in other nations. Repatriates often comment on Americans' insensitivity toward other cultures and lack of curiosity about the rest of the world, coupled with a tendency to make judgments about the morality (or lack of it) of the actions of other nations. Even returnees who describe themselves as conservative or "hawkish" believe that this "holier than thou" attitude is the underlying cause of the nation's unsatisfactory foreign relations. As one repatriate remarks, "Americans tend to think they are better than others and often don't have the courtesy to learn the language or the customs of the country they are dealing with."

For the Absentee American, this is a fundamental problem, and the solution is increased intercultural contact: "As an American who has lived most of my life overseas, I feel that talking with and exchanging thoughts and ideas with people on an everyday basis will always accomplish more toward understanding each other than any government official could ever hope to accomplish." Another returnee states the matter more simply: "More Americans should spend time abroad. The clichés are true."

A returnee who spent much of her childhood in Germany illustrates this point: "We found that the German people were generally very open to the Americans as long as Americans were polite and willing to try their life-style. The Europeans in general were intrigued by the Americans, especially those who attempted to assimilate into their culture, even if it was for a short period of time." Another repatriate notes that many Europeans did not like Americans, "mainly because they wouldn't learn local customs, language, and expected everyone to help them out all the time."

The need to learn and speak foreign languages is emphasized as a means of achieving greater intercultural understanding and respect. One repatriate notes that "we are barely teaching English here, to say nothing of foreign languages. Virtually every foreign visitor speaks English idiomatically or at least accurately, and many other languages besides, but we can't converse in anything but English." A returnee who is fluent in Portuguese, Spanish, and French comments that "the ability to be multilingual is barely accepted in the United States, and *expected* anywhere else in the world."

Many repatriates comment that Americans seem to be blind to the ethnocentric bias of the nation's relations with other cultures. As one returnee notes, "The United States suffers from the belief that all countries have to be the same as us to be good and we have a misguided need to change everyone else. Our failure to understand other cultures is resulting in our declining influence in the world." Another repatriate remarks, "Living abroad allowed me to see what others thought of the United States and gave me a chance to examine my own thoughts about the United States in a global context. I feel the United States has a global PR problem."

Returnees repeatedly emphasize that understanding other cultures is a prerequisite for appropriate foreign policy. As one repatriate expresses it, "Sometimes the United States tries to make other countries conform to what *we* think they should be rather than take the time to help the country develop in the best way for it." Repatriates often point out that whatever efforts are made to understand other cultures are generally superficial and biased. In the case of the Middle East, for example, repatriates feel that most Americans do not even begin to understand the Arabs' point of view and make no effort to do so.

Many Absentee Americans have developed a strong and realistic respect for democracy and believe that other nations would benefit from more democratic governance. For them it is particularly embarrassing to see the United States imposing its will on other nations by force rather than demonstrating through example how democracy works: "There was a time when the United States was looked on as an example of freedom and democracy. We should spend less time trying to influence other countries and let our basic good qualities serve as an example." These returnees believe that the American system is basically sound; they believe in it in principle even though they are ashamed of many aspects of U.S. foreign policy.

Their frustration is intensified by the feeling that the United States could play a leadership role in promoting international cooperation, yet in many instances it fails even to abide by international law, let alone recognize that cooperation is necessary for survival. Returnees would agree with Daniel Patrick Moynihan's contention, in *On the Law of Nations*, that adherence to international law is necessary as a means of ensuring safe and civilized behavior in the coming century, and that it is also the best way to promote democracy.

The sense of cultural relativity shared by most Absentee Americans leads them to believe that the United States could not only present a model of democracy and freedom but also learn a great deal from other nations: "Other countries can show us a few things. And we don't have all the answers."

A CHANGING WORLD ROLE

Some repatriates are concerned that the United States pours money into other nations for political purposes and pays insufficient attention to the problems of its own citizens. This view has both liberal and conservative elements. One repatriate remarks, "I feel we are losing ground as leaders in the world because of our unethical behavior and our superior attitude and how we give to everyone and never call in their debts. It makes us look like fools." Another says, "We don't spend our country's money wisely." A third, expressing a less common point of view, comments that other nations "are taking advantage of us by flooding our country with their products and buying our land and businesses."

The socialization of "military brats" includes an emphasis on patriotism and a belief that the United States should play a leadership role. Although Absentee Americans from military families express as great a variety of views as other returnees, they are more likely to express dismay at the nation's inability to maintain or enhance its superpower role and to feel that other nations are taking advantage of American generosity or lack of forcefulness. A returnee whose Air Force family was stationed in Japan and Germany during her childhood expresses this point of view: "Until recently the United States has been a leader in the contemporary world, the 'gold standard' against which other countries measured themselves in military, economic, technological, and educational areas, and general standard of living. However, I fear our leadership is not taken for granted anymore and we've been slipping from 'first place' for many years, perhaps for even a generation. I think national greed and materialism has drastically undermined the ideals and precepts on which this country was founded. As a country I feel we are self-oriented, not concerned about the welfare of fellow Americans, much less oppressed poor people of other nations. We are a country in dire need of *internal* healing. Other countries know this, and it can't help but affect our clout in the community of nations."

Another repatriate from a military family states this view more succintly: "I feel, unfortunately, that we are going downhill in our power as a nation, just like the Roman and other kingdoms."

John Littlefield, an Air Force Security Police officer whose father also served in the Air Force, offers the following explanation for the nation's declining world role: "We are extremely sheltered as a country and isolationist in our attitude. We have no borders that melt one culture with another as in Europe." Another returnee points out that "the United States could learn much from the thousands of years' experience that European culture and society have to offer."

Some returnees feel that the United States' world role is undergoing a major change—a feeling that intensified as this book was being written and Eastern Europe and the Soviet Union underwent immense political, economic, and social upheavals. "This is a time of transition for U.S. influence abroad," says one repatriate. "Despite our enormous wealth, the decline of U.S. economic influence internationally is causing many Americans to reevaluate our commitments abroad." For some, this change is inevitable but is occurring too slowly. But even returnees who feel that the United States is still a leader in the Western world express doubt about whether it should be *the* leader. Repatriates often express the hope that the United States will join in voluntary, cooperative efforts to address global economic and environmental problems: "We have to work with other peoples/countries to a common goal" is a typical comment.

Rebecca Sholes sums up the feelings of many repatriates in the following comments: "The role of the United States in the contemporary world has drastically changed in the last decade, and I feel that it is time we reevaluated our foreign policy and developed new and more innovative ways of dealing with world problems. We should no longer play the role of the world's policeman, often acting from some moralistic point of view that is not always well defined. As a nation, we have a tendency to get involved in regional conflicts without understanding their cultural and political complexities, a tendency that has serious negative consequences both for ourselves and for the other countries involved. Our government needs to learn to be one of the negotiators in a world political crisis, not the sole one. Our political culture and way of life is not the only viable one and we need to be better able to negotiate and find middle paths to peaceful solutions."

Another repatriate points out that the United States' post–World War II ascendancy was bound to end because Americans "came to assume that our economic might and military superiority were internationally recognized birthrights, which they are not." He adds, "We have lapsed into mediocrity (probably irreversibly) unless we wake up, get to know the rest of the planet as we never have before, and resolve to reenergize our work ethic, our inventive spirit, our optimism, and our creative responses to a changing world."

Returnees often say that they respect and admire the United States for its efforts to help other nations: "We do a lot for other nations at our expense." They note, however, that the United States' altruism is often coupled with naivete and/or ethnocentrism. In their view, many of the difficulties encountered by the foreign-aid program arise because "we seem to assume that other people think and act as we do." There are also problems stemming from the fact that aid has become increasingly tied to national political and military objectives. Some repatriates are concerned about the apparent dependence of many nations on the United States. Others note that U.S. "help" may sometimes be indistinguishable from interference. It is widely agreed that more grassroots involvement—through the Peace Corps, for example—would be more effective.

The Absentee American's view of U.S. assistance is illustrated by the following comment: "I like the idea of the United States helping other nations. But it should be done within the realms of their culture and ways. I believe U.S. citizens going to other nations should know and understand that country's culture and shape their life-style to the country's culture (as much as possible), plus learn the language and realize we are a guest. If other countries do not want our aid, we should cease giving it. The United States is a great nation and for the most part, very caring and concerned. But we tend to feel all other countries should be like us."

Returnees also emphasize that social and economic problems within the United States are crying out for attention: "We have enough going on right here to keep us occupied for a century." This view is coupled with the feeling that domestic problems will weaken the nation internationally. As one returnee says, "We are divided as a people, uncertain of our direction and goals, and we may be losing our preeminent position in the world." Another repatriate notes that "unless we repair our own home (our education is poor, our drug problems terrifying), we cannot pretend that others will perceive us in a leadership role: nor can we pretend to help others stabilize their 'homes.' "

There is concern about the amount and nature of the assistance the United States offers to other nations. Many returnees believe that nations that have developed stable economies and become world powers in their own right, such as Germany and Japan, should share the responsibility for maintaining order and economic progress throughout the world. "The United States still thinks that we need to keep control on the world in order to stay on top, but no one nation can do that any longer," says one. Another notes, "We can't foot the bill for protecting Japan and Germany's oil supply any longer."

Many Absentee Americans emphasize the need for sharing rather than giving, except in the case of extremely poor nations. Joan Halbert, an executive assistant who spent her teenage years in Brazil, expresses this view as follows: "America is the strongest nation on earth and I believe we should continue to provide assistance where needed and share our collective wealth and intellect with other less fortunate nations, in the vein of 'teach a man how to fish' rather than 'give a man a fish.' " There is also general agreement that the U.S. role in other nations should be humanistic and ethical rather than militaristic and acquisitive. Many repatriates feel that the most important role the United States could play in the future would be to support cooperative efforts to attack global environmental problems.

Joseph Boling, the son of an Air Force officer and now an Army officer himself, sums up this feeling: "I get tired of being dumped on by other countries not willing to solve their own problems, but I also see Americans as somewhat arrogant, intolerant, and unwilling to accept the fact that others can work harder and be more successful than we. I do not feel that we should protect inefficient industries or get indignant when others deliver better products at lower cost. I favor gradual reduction of our world-policing role—let the rest of the Western world foot the bill for their own security."

Repatriates often comment on the competitive attitude of most Americans toward the rest of the world. They do not understand the dismay expressed by many Americans at the idea that another nation might become the world's dominant economic power, or the widespread belief that it is somehow sinful for companies based in other countries to be more successful than American firms in U.S. markets. They do not deny the nation's leadership potential, but they do not feel that it is necessary for the United States to be number one in all things.

These divergent views point up once again the duality that is characteristic of the attitudes of Absentee Americans. This duality can be seen in the comments of a returnee who says she feels "torn. At times I feel we should let other countries flounder in their problems [but] I also think we should try to help them militarily, also medically—especially the children of Third-World nations." Another repatriate expresses this duality as follows: "I still feel the United States has a place as a peace-keeping nation (a mediator), but I no longer feel like we are everybody's babysitter. I still feel we should help when asked, or when human rights are blatantly being abused. Helping does not always mean sending in the Marines." A third returnee describes Americans as naive and selfish, yet approves of the nation's "essential guts." Others say that the nation is "well-meaning but ineffective," or "like a naive adolescent—good at heart, but wrapped up in its own problems."

NEED FOR GLOBAL VISION

Despite these apparently contradictory views, most Absentee Americans agree that the United States lacks a global vision. In their view, vast natural resources and a high level of living have the effect of causing the nation to remain insulated and isolated from the rest of the world. Americans who have not lived abroad often resemble the man who was unconcerned when the rowboat he shared with another man sprang a leak. "I'm not worried," he said; "it's your end of the boat that's sinking." Nontraveled Americans tend to view the United States as wholly separate from the rest of the world, an ocean away not only physically but politically and culturally and sometimes even economically. Absentee Americans, in contrast, develop a view of the world as a tight-knit, interdependent set of nations and peoples. They tend to see the United States as just one of a large number of sovereign nations, all of which are significant to world affairs. They are concerned about the United States' tendency to make assumptions about its importance in the world that cause resentment in other countries, and about the attitude of "natural superiority" that permeates its dealings with other nations.

This viewpoint is largely a matter of perspective. To the Absentee American, all countries, including the United States, are more or less "foreign." By the same token, any country can be "home." Relations between nations therefore are not a question of "we" and "they," our interests versus theirs. They are, or should be, a question of making arrangements that are satisfactory and beneficial to all. This point of view is summarized in the following comments: "I view the United States as one member of the world community, not the center of the universe. Often I think we are more influential than we have right to be, and we operate on an 'ends justify the means' basis like the rest of the world, despite patriotic denials." "The United States is just one country among many—not always the wisest or the strongest. We should use our wealth and strength to help others in need, but never to dominate or control."

Other repatriates suggest that the United States could continue to exercise leadership as a model of democracy, but that it must enter into economic partnerships with other nations and do more to solve its own domestic problems: "We must be a responsible force in world politics, but we need to tend our home fires as well."

Absentee Americans agree that the U.S. role in the world is changing. In their view, the United States is losing its dominant position, whether measured in military, political, or economic terms, but this is not necessarily a bad thing. Other nations can play leadership roles as well. From the standpoint of the repatriate, this should be viewed as an opportunity, not as a threat.

9

CROSSING BOUNDARIES

All of us are from somewhere else . . .

For Absentee Americans, the tearing down of the Berlin Wall was an event with both real and symbolic significance. The wall had long stood as a symbol of artifical division. In the view of many repatriates, national boundaries also create artificial divisions. Like the interior walls of a house, they are necessary but need not constitute impenetrable barriers. People can communicate with others in the house even if they happen to be in different rooms. Similarly, from the perspective of Absentee Americans, although national boundaries cannot be eliminated—at least not yet—their symbolic importance can be reduced or modified. This, they feel, is an essential goal that needs to be taken more seriously as the twentieth century draws to a close.

Underlying this view of nations is the repatriate's view of individuals as wholly distinct from the groups or categories of which they are members. Although returnees are highly aware of the differences among individuals, at the same time they are acutely aware of the similarities among human beings everywhere, regardless of nationality. Absentee Americans are bemused by the emphasis on ethnic and racial differences that pervades American culture; to them, such differences, while noticed, are insignificant. In their view, the United States is a microcosm of the world as a whole, in which people from diverse origins need to work together toward common goals.

In the Absentee American can be seen the intersection of nationality with cultural relativity. Repatriates have lived as Americans in other cultures, where being an American was central to their identity, and they have lived as quasi-Americans in the United States, striving to find an identity in a culture that is at once familiar and utterly alien. This experience has a variety of long-term effects, of which two are especially significant: It causes repatriates to become strongly attached to the ideals of America while at the same time feeling distant from American culture and critical of certain aspects of it. It also causes them to view U.S. foreign relations through the wrong end of a telescope; they know from firsthand experience how America and its policies appear to people in other nations.

In the opinion of many repatriates, recent events appear to signal a change in the relationship between the United States and other nations. Those who grew up in Europe during the cold war express relief at the apparent end of that confrontation. They also see evidence that American leaders are beginning to show more sensitivity to the political autonomy of countries in Europe and the Pacific basin. Indeed, many returnees believe that the United States is evolving toward a new pattern of behavior that takes account of the interconnectedness of nations. In their view, economic and environmental issues will inevitably lead to a more cooperative approach to other nations. "We can't be Lone Rangers any more," says one. "We are dependent on the rest of the world." However, when asked their views on the U.S. role in the Persian Gulf war, several repatriates stated that the United States was still taking direct rather than collective action. Moreover, they expressed the belief that the underlying motivation was still self-interest rather than a genuine desire to enter into partnership with other nations.

In the view of Absentee Americans, a fundamental problem with the attitude of many nontraveled Americans toward the rest of the world is the feeling of superiority with which they look upon other cultures. They are troubled by the widely held belief that the United States is the greatest nation in the world and that, by extension, its people are superior to all others. People of other nations are variously viewed as dependent on the United States for protection, as a pool of cheap labor, or as inferior in other ways; at best, they are seen as "quaint" or "interesting." Repatriates emphasize that until this national superiority complex is tempered with a more genuine appreciation of the actual or potential greatness of other nations and peoples, little lasting progress can be made toward mutually beneficial relations with other nations.

Above all, Absentee Americans see a need for pragmatism (not to be confused with self-interest) in the nation's interactions with others. They point out, for example, that people in other nations continue to believe that the United States has unlimited resources, even though it has become a debtor nation and its traditional generosity cannot continue unabated. Returnees do not deny that the United States has an important role to play on the world stage, but they believe that role needs to be redefined on the basis of practical considerations rather than ideology. As one repatriate puts it, "I believe we are trying to do too much and are not doing very well. We need to let our allies absorb some of the many roles. By doing fewer things but doing them very well our image will improve." Another points to the need for "more humane, but also more realistic" policies.

At the same time, Absentee Americans see a need for greater vision, for a need to look ahead and plan for a future in which nations will interact in a more cooperative manner. Many point to the Peace Corps and student exchange programs like

Youth for Understanding as examples of the kind of visionary, yet pragmatic, intercultural experience that should receive greater emphasis in the future.

In addition, the consensus is that a change in orientation must occur in the schools and must focus on the next generation. Returnees frequently describe American education as provincial and call for greater curricular emphasis on foreign languages and cultures, more extensive exchange programs, and other programs focusing on intercultural understanding. Many note the need to teach a less ethnocentric and xenophobic view of the world, to teach Americans to feel that they are a part of the world, not apart from it. Few believe that such a transformation in attitudes can occur overnight. Instead, they express the hope for a reformed educational system that prepares young people to participate intelligently in the international community.

Repatriates themselves have the potential to serve as a valuable resource in achieving this goal. By training and inclination, many are equipped to act as intercultural mediators. A mediating person "has systematic knowledge of more than one culture; . . . has skills that enable him to overcome the barriers to communication between actors from different cultural backgrounds; . . . has a humanitarian concern for the well-being of the people he is mediating between; respects the indigenous values of the societies he is operating in; and . . . is concerned with preserving the core aspects of the cultural systems undergoing social change."[1] Although exposure to more than one culture as a child does not automatically create a skilled mediator, Absentee Americans often serve as "culture bridges," helping people from different cultures recognize their commonalities and understand their differences. The experience of repatriation has made them flexible in their thinking, a quality that should be in greater demand as the need to cross cultural bridges becomes more evident. Many are employed in "bridging" occupations—as teachers, consultants, trainers, counselors—positions that allow them to add their global perspective to the processes through which ideas and ideals are communicated. Finally, their appreciation of American ideals, coupled with their critical perspective on U.S. foreign policy, enables them to participate intelligently in policy debates. They represent a force for cosmopolitanism in a nation with a marked tendency toward provincialism.

No longer the undisputed leader of the world community, the United States needs to reassess its role in world affairs; at the same time, Americans need to modify their attitudes toward people of other nations. This process is already under way: The ugly American is being replaced by the worldly American. And in the vanguard are the generations of Americans who spent their childhood years in other countries—the Absentee Americans. They are the prototypes of the international citizen of the twenty-first century.

NOTE

1. Stephen Bochner, *The Mediating Person* (Boston: G. K. Hall, 1981), p. 207.

APPENDIX A:
THE QUESTIONNAIRE

Interested readers are invited to complete the questionnaire and send it to the author at 38–15 Corporal Kennedy St., Bayside, NY 11361.

Name:_____ Age:_____

Address:_____ Place of Birth:_____

_____

_____ Phone:_____

Occupation:_____

1. Where did you live during your childhood years (0-18)?

_____

_____

_____

2. What were your parents' or guardians' occupations while overseas?

_____

_____

3. To what extent and in what ways did you participate in the life of the American community there?

_____

_____

_____

4. To what extent did you learn the language and participate in the culture of the country or countries in which you were stationed?

_____

_____

_____

5. How old were you when you returned to the United States to live?

_____

6. If you returned to the United States after an absence of many years, how did you respond emotionally to the "reentry" experience, and how did others respond to you?

_____

_____

_____

_____

_____

7. Do you feel that you are well integrated into American society?
Why or why not?

_____

_____

_____

_____

_____

8. In what ways do you think the experience of living overseas has
influenced your beliefs and attitudes? Are there other factors, such
as ethnic, racial, or bilingual/bicultural background, that played a
part in your reaction to life overseas?

_____

_____

_____

_____

_____

9. How do you feel about the role of the United States in the
contemporary world?

_____

_____

_____

_____

_____

10. Do you readily identify yourself as "an American"? If so, what
does this signify to you? If not, how do you view yourself?

_____

_____

_____

_____

_____

APPENDIX B:
ORGANIZATIONS OF
INTEREST TO
REPATRIATES

The following organizations offer publications and other programs of interest to Absentee Americans and others concerned with intercultural communication.

Global Nomads International
P.O. Box 9584
Washington, DC 20016-9584

> A not-for-profit association dedicated to providing opportunities for global nomads to explore, affirm, and act on their unique international experience for their own enrichment and that of the larger world community.

Mu Kappa International
P.O. Box 1388
De Soto, TX 75115

> A fraternal association whose purpose is to help missionary kids in their cultural transitions and to promote growth, unity, and Christian fellowship among chapter members.

Overseas Schools Combined Alumni Registry (OSCAR)
P.O. Box 7763
Washington, DC 20044

> A central registry for students who attended American junior and senior high schools outside the United States, along with their teachers and parents; includes schools run by the Department of Defense.

Overseas Brats
P.O. Box 29805
San Antonio, TX 78229

> A nonprofit organization of overseas alumni comprising former dependents of U.S. military, government, and civilian personnel; assists in referring overseas alumni to their respective reunion committees or organizations.

Society for Intercultural Education, Training and Research
808 17th St. N.W., Suite 200
Washington, DC 20006

> An interdisciplinary professional and service organization whose purpose is to implement and promote cooperative interactions and effective communication among peoples of diverse cultures, races, and ethnic groups.

BIBLIOGRAPHY

Austin, Clyde N., ed. *Cross-Cultural Re-entry: A Book of Readings.* Abilene, Texas: Abilene Christian University Press, 1986.

Barnett, Vincent M., ed. *The Representation of the United States Abroad*, rev. ed. New York: Praeger, 1965.

Blancké, W. Wendell. *The Foreign Service of the United States.* New York: Praeger, 1969.

Bloomfield, Katherine M. *The Impact of Overseas Living on Adolescent Identity Formation.* Northampton, Mass.: Smith College School for Social Work, 1983.

Bochner, Stephen. *The Mediating Person: Bridges Between Cultures.* Boston: G. K. Hall, 1981.

Camus, Albert. *The Stranger.* Trans. Stuart Gilbert. New York: Knopf, 1946.

Dodd, C. H., and F. F. Montalvo, eds. *Intercultural Skills for Multicultural Societies.* Washington, D.C.: International Society for Intercultural Education, Training, and Research, 1985.

Eakin, Kay Branaman. *The Foreign Service Teenager—At Home in the U.S.: A Few Thoughts for Parents Returning with Teenagers.* Washington, D.C.: Overseas Briefing Center, Foreign Service

Institute, U.S. Department of State, May 1988.

Hale, Edward E. *The Man Without a Country*. Boston: Roberts Brothers, 1897.

Herman, Simon N., and Erling O. Schild. "The Stranger-Group in a Cross-Cultural Situation." *Sociometry, 24* (1961): 165–76.

Hirsch, E. D., Jr. *Cultural Literacy: What Every American Needs to Know*. Boston: Houghton Mifflin, 1987.

Hirsch, E. D., Jr., Joseph F. Kett, and James Trefil. *The Dictionary of Cultural Literacy: What Every American Needs to Know*. Boston: Houghton Mifflin, 1988.

Kittredge, Claire. "Growing up Global." *Boston Globe Magazine*, April 3, 1988.

Lambert, Richard D., ed. *Americans Abroad (Annals of the American Academy of Political and Social Sciences), 368* (November 1966).

Lewis, Tom J., and Robert E. Jungman, eds. *On Being Foreign: Culture Shock in Short Fiction*. Yarmouth, Maine: Intercultural Press, 1986.

Merrill-Foster, R. J. "Strangers in Their Own Land." Unpublished manuscript, 1986. Available from R. J. Merrill-Foster, "Les Bois"—Stinson Lake, Rumney, NH 03266–9801.

Miller, R. F. "Where Do You Come From? Growing Up in the Foreign Service." *Department of State Newsletter*, April 1974.

Nash, Dennison. *A Community in Limbo: An Anthropological Study of an American Community Abroad*. Bloomington: Indiana University Press, 1970.

Pollock, David C. "Transition Experience: A Model of Reentry" (October 1987). Available from D. C. Pollock, Rt. 1, Box 23, Centerville Rd., Houghton, NY 14744.

Schutz, Alfred. "The Stranger: An Essay in Social Psychology" and "The Homecomer." In *Collected Papers*, Vol. II: *Studies in Social Theory*, ed. Arvid Brodersen. The Hague: Martinus Nijhoff, 1964.

Simmel, Georg. "The Stranger." In *The Sociology of Georg Simmel*, trans. and ed. Kurt H. Wolff. New York: Free Press, 1950.

Steigman, Andrew L. *The Foreign Service of the United States: First Line of Defense*. Boulder, Colo.: Westview Press, 1985.

Stonequist, Everett V. *The Marginal Man: A Study in Personality and Culture Conflict*. New York: Russell and Russell, 1937.

Tooley, K. "The Role of Geographic Mobility in Some Adjustment Problems of Children and Families." *Journal of the American Academy of Child Psychology, 9* (1970): 366–78.

Torbiorn, I. *Living Abroad: Personal Adjustment and Personnel Policy in the Overseas Setting.* New York: Wiley, 1982.

Tsung, L. C. *The Marginal Man.* New York: Pageant Press, 1963.

Useem, John. "Work Patterns of Americans in India." *Annals of the American Academy of Political and Social Sciences, 368* (1966): 146–56.

Useem, Ruth Hill. "The American Family in India." *Annals of the American Academy of Political and Social Sciences, 368* (1966): 132–45.

Useem, Ruth Hill, and Richard D. Downie. "Third-Culture Kids." *Today's Education* (September-October 1976): 103–5.

Van Reken, Ruth. *Letters Never Sent.* Oakbrook, Ill.: Darwill, 1984.

Ward, Ted. *Living Overseas: A Book of Preparations.* New York: Free Press, 1984.

Werkman, S. "A Heritage of Transience: Psychological Effects of Growing Up Overseas." In *The Child in His Family,* Vol. 5, ed. E. J. Anthony and C. Chilaud. New York: Wiley, 1978.

Wilson, Angene H. "Returned Exchange Students: Becoming Mediating Persons." *International Journal of Intercultural Relations, 9* (1985): 285–304.

Winfield, Louise. *Living Overseas.* Washington, D.C.: Public Affairs Press, 1962.

INDEX

ABOUT THE AUTHOR

CAROLYN DOGGETT SMITH grew up in a Foreign Service family in the late 1940s and 1950s. She has lived in Italy, Greece, Switzerland, Pakistan, and Vietnam and now works as a textbook editor and freelance writer in New York City. Her other publications include *In the Field: Readings on the Field Research Experience* and *The Healing Experience: Readings on the Social Context of Health Care.*